The Writing on the Wall

Peter Kruschwitz is Professor of Classics at the University of Reading and Fellow of the Pontifical Academy for Latin. He is a specialist in Latin language and literature, especially of the Roman Republican period, and he has published extensively on ancient Latin inscriptions. Born in 1973 in Berlin, he moved to Reading in 2007 and has since developed a keen interest in the remarkable history of this town.

Also published by Two Rivers Press:

Caught on Camera by Terry Allsop
Plant Portraits by Post by Julia Trickey
Allen W. Seaby: Art and nature by Martin Andrews & Robert Gillmor
Reading Detectives by Kerry Renshaw
Fox Talbot & the Reading Establishment by Martin Andrews
Cover Birds by Robert Gillmor
All Change at Reading: The Railway and the Station 1840–2013
   by Adam Sowan
An Artist's Year in the Harris Garden by Jenny Halstead
Caversham Court Gardens: A Heritage Guide
   by Friends of Caversham Court Gardens
Believing in Reading: Our Places of Worship by Adam Sowan
Newtown: A Photographic Journey in Reading 1974 by Terry Allsop
Bikes, Balls & Biscuitmen: Our Sporting Life
   by Tim Crooks & Reading Museum
Birds, Blocks & Stamps: Post & Go Birds of Britain by Robert Gillmor
The Reading Quiz Book by Adam Sowan
Bizarre Berkshire: An A–Z Guide by Duncan Mackay
Broad Street Chapel & the Origins of Dissent in Reading by Geoff Sawers
Reading Poetry: An Anthology edited by Peter Robinson
Reading: A Horse-Racing Town by Nigel Sutcliffe
Eat Wild by Duncan MacKay
Down by the River: The Thames and Kennet in Reading by Gillian Clark
A Much-maligned Town: Opinions of Reading 1126–2008
   by Adam Sowan
A Mark of Affection: The Soane Obelisk in Reading by Adam Sowan
The Stranger in Reading edited by Adam Sowan
The Holy Brook by Adam Sowan
Charms against Jackals edited by Adam Stout and Geoff Sawers
Abattoirs Road to Zinzan Street by Adam Sowan

The Writing on the Wall
Reading's Latin Inscriptions

Peter Kruschwitz

TWO
RIVERS
PRESS

First published in the UK in 2015 by Two Rivers Press
7 Denmark Road, Reading RG1 5PA
www.tworiverspress.com

The author wishes to thank the following for permission to
reproduce digital images. For the photos on p.45 (*Reading Mercury*
banner) and p.50 (Silchester clay tile) I acknowledge Reading Museum,
Reading Borough Council (all rights reserved); for the photos on p.41
(Roman clay lamp) and p.73 (Roman tombstone from Leptis Magna)
I acknowledge the Ure Museum of Greek Archaeology, University of
Reading (all rights reserved).

ISBN 978-1-901677-99-7

1 2 3 4 5 6 7 8 9

Two Rivers Press is represented in the UK by Inpress Ltd
and distributed by Central Books.

Cover design by Nadja Guggi with illustrations by Peter Hay
Text design by Nadja Guggi and typeset in Parisine

Printed and bound in Great Britain by Imprint Digital, Exeter.

Acknowledgements

I wish to thank those wonderful people and institutions of Reading who gave me generous access to their premises, collections, and archives, and without whom this anthology could not have materialised: Fr. David A Harris (St Giles-in-Reading); Rev'd. Canon Brian Shenton (Reading Minster); Rev'd. Canon Christopher Russell, Sheena Littlehale, and Claire Brown (St Laurence's); Sandie Blair Bonner (Mayor's Office, Reading), Myfanwy Giddings and Christine Kattirtzi (Kendrick School); Gillian Greenaway (Reading Museum); Guja Bandini, Fred Davis, and Amy Smith (University of Reading).

Sally Mortimore and the team of Two Rivers Press have done a splendid job in turning my pile of unorganised, random notes into a beautifully produced book.

I am indebted to the following for their support and advice (in alphabetical order): Orazio Camaioni, Virginia L. Campbell, Juan Francisco Fraile Vicente, Jane F. Gardner, Myfanwy Giddings, Emma Holding, Brian Kemp, Gill Knight, Paola Nasti, Matthew Nicholls, Clare Nukui, Peter Robinson, Ian Rutherford, Kim Shahabudin, and Anika and Paul Strobach.

I dedicate this book to Jane F. Gardner. Her stupendous, wide-ranging learning, as well as her infallible judgement, are constant sources of inspiration and envy to me.

Contents

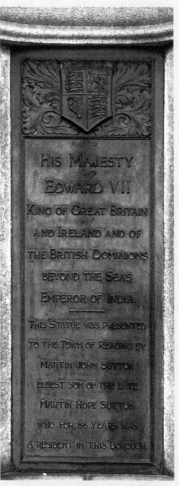

HIS MAJESTY
EDWARD VII
KING OF GREAT BRITAIN
AND IRELAND AND OF
THE BRITISH DOMINIONS
BEYOND THE SEAS
EMPEROR OF INDIA.

THIS STATUE WAS PRESENTED
TO THE TOWN OF READING BY
MARTIN JOHN SUTTON
ELDEST SON OF THE LATE
MARTIN HOPE SUTTON
WHO FOR 86 YEARS WAS
A RESIDENT IN THIS BOROUGH.

The Latin Inscriptions of Reading: An Introduction

Welcome to Reading (or: a Greeting from the Past)

A monumental statue of King Edward VII, situated on a roundabout just outside the train station, greets visitors to Reading arriving by train or coach. The statue, sculpted by George Edward Wade, was erected in 1902, a time when the British Empire was at the very peak of its expansion. It shows the king with his crown, an orb, sceptre, and lavish garments, standing on an ornate pedestal.

Some may well be able to recognise this ruler and may even be able to guess why this statue had been erected in Reading. For those wanting the facts, a set of three inscriptions explains all this in detail.

At the front of the pedestal, a large metal plaque names the person honoured as well as the benefactor:

His Majesty
Edward VII
King of Great Britain
and Ireland and of
the British Dominions
beyond the Seas
Emperor of India

———

This Statue was presented
to the Town of Reading by
Martin John Sutton
eldest son of the late
Martin Hope Sutton
who for 66 Years was
a resident in this Borough.

CORONATION
OF
HIS MAJESTY KING EDWARD VII
1902.

RECORD OF THE
COMMEMORATIVE CELEBRATIONS
AND PUBLIC REJOICINGS HELD
IN THE COUNTY BOROUGH OF READING.
DINNER TO 2000 AGED POOR PERSONS.
TEA TO 14,500 SCHOOL CHILDREN.
SPECIAL SERVICES AT
CHURCHES AND CHAPELS.
PROCESSION OF THE TOWN COUNCIL,
AND OF ODDFELLOWS, FORESTERS, AND
OTHER BENEFIT AND FRIENDLY SOCIETIES.
TRADE, FLORALLY DECORATED, EMBLEMATIC,
AND HISTORICAL CARS, AND
DECORATED CARRIAGES, INCLUDING
AUTOMOBILES AND CYCLES.
AQUATIC SPORTS, AMATEUR & NON AMATEUR
AND OLD ENGLISH SPORTS.
WATER CARNIVAL WITH PROCESSION OF
ILLUMINATED AND DECORATED BOATS
AND STEAM LAUNCHES.
ROYAL SALUTE.
PLANTING COMMEMORATION TREE IN THE
FORBURY PLEASURE GROUNDS
BY THE MAYORESS.
ILLUMINATED PROMENADE CONCERTS.
TORCHLIGHT PROCESSION ATTENDED BY THE
MAYOR AND BY THE CHAIRMEN AND
SECRETARIES OF THE CORONATION COMMITTEES.
DISTRIBUTION OF MEDALS AND CORONATION
PICTURES BY THE MAYOR & THE MAYORESS.

ALFRED HOLLAND BULL, J.P. MAYOR.
HENRY DAY, TOWN CLERK.

On the opposite side, facing the town centre, a longer inscription provides considerable detail about the occasion on which the statue was erected:

Coronation
of
His Majesty King Edward VII
1902.

———

Record of the
Commemorative Celebrations
and Public Rejoicings held
in the County Borough of Reading.

———

Dinner to 2000 Aged Poor Persons.
Tea to 14,500 School Children
Special Services at
Churches and Chapels.
Procession of the Town Council
and of Oddfellows, Foresters, and
other Benefit and Friendly Societies;
Trade, Florally Decorated, Emblematic,
and Historical Cars, and
Decorated Carriages, including
Automobiles and Cycles.
Aquatic Sports, Amateur & Non Amateur
and Old English Sports,
Water Carnival with procession of
illuminated and decorated boats
and steam launches.
Royal Salute.
Planting Commemorative Tree in the
Forbury Pleasure Grounds
by the Mayoress,
Illuminated Promenade Concerts.
Torchlight Procession Attended by the
Mayor and by the Chairmen and
Secretaries of the Coronation Committees.
Distribution of Medals and Coronation
Pictures by the Mayor & the Mayoress.

———

Alfred Holland Bull J.P. Mayor.
Henry Day, Town Clerk.

And then there is a third inscription – short, seemingly insignificant, and easily overlooked. It runs just below the king's feet:

Unlike the other two inscriptions, this one is not written in English, though at first glance it may appear to be. It is in Latin, although much abbreviated. The inscription, with its abbreviations resolved, reads:

Edward(us) VII R(ex) I(mperator)

which translates as
'Edward VII, King–Emperor.'

This one example raises several questions. What is the purpose of this statue and its inscriptions? And why is one of the inscriptions written in Latin? Why this one in particular?

It also opens up wider questions. What is Latin doing in the inscriptions of Reading anyway? What makes it different or special? What is the point of communicating in a language that few people can understand?

This book will answer these questions and many more. It offers a fascinating range of texts and translations, chosen from the wealth of Reading's Latin inscriptions. Starting from the statue of King Edward VII with its Latin and English inscriptions, it will take you on a journey of discovery, a mystery tour through the remarkable and chequered history of this town. It will uncover some of Reading's hidden treasures, and it will bring back to light individuals who have contributed to the extraordinary history of this town. Finally, it will raise awareness of how important it is to understand, preserve, and appreciate the rich heritage and the memory of a town that has a lot to be proud of.

In order to add meaning to our journey, we need to answer a few preliminary questions. What are inscriptions, and what do they have to tell us? How should we study them? Why should we listen to their stories, and is there anything we need to be aware of? Are inscriptions different from other types of text?

We start on familiar ground, with inscriptions written (mostly) in English.

Monuments, Inscriptions, and Memory

Contrary to what you might expect, monuments are not really for those who are commemorated by them. They are for the living, for those who may see and interact with them. The word 'monument', from Latin *monumentum*, literally means 'reminder', 'something that perpetuates remembrance'.

Using our introductory example, of what does the statue of King Edward VII remind us? Is the message that we receive from this monument still the same as it was for those people who first saw it, more than 110 years ago? Does it send out a single message, consistent and unchanged across time, or is it a way for any generation to reflect on the ever changing times and spaces that we live in?

The message sent out by the monument of King Edward VII could be saying many things. Is it an expression of subjects' lasting appreciation for the long-standing tradition of their monarchy? Is it an expression of historical awareness? Is it a homage to an age when Britain was a rather different place, an empire, with provinces across the globe, asserting its pride and celebrating its rule, epitomised by the clear assertion of male dominance and power in a proud, male king-emperor? Is it an offending, offensive object, for all the same reasons? Could it, despite the presence of the monarch, be seen as a monument to civic pride?

It is unlikely that there is any consensus about this, or that there ever was. To the motorist, the statue, with its peculiar position in the roundabout, is hardly more than an indication of where to turn. To those arranging a meeting place or giving directions, it may be a useful landmark. To those in a hurry to get into town from the station, the statue may simply be yet another monumental British monarch, obstructing the landscape and blocking direct access to the town centre.

Your opinions of the monument are likely to change, or become more complex, once you take account the inscriptions that form part of the monument and therefore part of an overall interpretation of it. The front plaque gives the name and titulature of the person commemorated, the *honorand*. At the same time, and, more importantly, it also mentions the benefactor(s), Martin John Sutton, and his late father, Martin Hope Sutton, who presented this statue to the town. It even mentions the father's long-term residency in Reading, clearly something the family took pride in.

This alone could prove the point that even this one statue was not merely a token of appreciation of, or an expression of hope in, the newly crowned king. It was also about the opportunity of the Suttons, Reading's famous suppliers of seeds and other horticultural products, to give something back to a community that they felt strongly about – to such an extent that they decided to make their names visible to the public, equally monumentally as the monarch's.

Another, additional message comes across through the inscriptions: a lengthy, most remarkable and detailed catalogue of public celebrations held in 1902 on the occasion of Edward's coronation, even listing the names of the mayor of Reading and the town clerk. If the record is to be trusted, the people of Reading celebrated the new king's coronation lavishly. If this was the case, then the statue may have been a powerful reminder of a glorious time to those who saw it erected in 1902.

Inscriptions and the Study of History

Inscriptions can be a powerful and immediate way to establish intellectual links with the past, not least due to the great variety of texts that fall into this category and the variety of individuals and institutions that have been instrumental in accumulating the multitude of inscriptions over time. The seemingly random nature of those inscriptions, thinned by a history that eventually tends to forget those who helped shape it, introduces us to a host of individuals and events that occasionally almost seem to have fallen out of a time warp.

Unlike history books that provide a narrative of events, inscriptions give a punctual, selective, skewed account of the past, with little or no regard to what really mattered or what made a difference. Inscriptions supplement written historical accounts, and they have the potential to provide an insight into people's lives, events, and values that cannot be derived from any other sources.

Inscriptions are historical documents. But does that mean that one should trust an inscription, and take it at face value? Are inscriptions an objective and unbiased record, as their lasting nature might suggest? They are certainly a monumental expression of what a dedicator wanted to commit to memory; that dedicator would have had a reason to do so, and possibly an agenda or an ideology, knowing that, accurate or not, inscriptions soon become part of the public record, and thus constitute archival truth – truth because it is written down for people to believe.

What does that mean? The inscription on the statue of King Edward VII that specifies in great detail public events and joyous occasions is not only a list. Items such as the dinner for 2,000 aged poor people or 14,500 school children are too even to be more than just ball-park figures, and they are too detailed to be just innocent accounts: they epitomise a financial engagement of a certain proportion, and they are meant to constitute a mutual obligation.

The mutual nature of such obligations, implied and represented through the public display of monumental inscriptions, may not always be obvious. Yet it exists, and the workings of this double obligation can also be seen on a remarkable, ornate inscription in Reading. In Castle Street, opposite the Police Station, there is a gateway leading towards two beautiful terraces of almshouses. To the right of the entrance, mounted on the wall of the right row of terraced houses, there is an old inscription, included here for a couple of Latin phrases that have been part of the English language for so long that they are not normally felt to be foreign by the majority of the population:

S(i)r Thomas Vachel, K(nigh)t (Bachelor)
erected these Alms-Houses
Anno Dom(ini) 1634 and endow'd
them with Forty Pounds p(er) Annum
for ever for the Maintenance of
Six poor Men.

Why attach such a plaque to these buildings? The obvious answer is to commemorate the donation, possibly with a desire to secure public acclaim for the benefactor. The text achieves a lot more, though; it mentions an exact sum of money for the endowment, it mentions its annual recurrence, and it mentions the open-endedness of the arrangement. These aspects again may be seen as stressing the generosity of the benefaction, benefitting the benefactor. More importantly, however, the publication of the details of this arrangement through public display creates undisputable evidence and a point of reference for those who wish to refer to an entitlement: no-one can now easily claim that there were only thirty-nine pounds available, or that funding was supposed to run out after just five years.

The power and binding force of this obligation can be seen from the fact that this inscription is still on display, albeit at a terrace of houses that have virtually nothing to do with the original Vachel almshouses in Reading! The original structure 'situated on the South side of Castle-street, near Pinkney-lane' was demolished in 1867 and replaced with the present terraces, funded with the proceeds of the sale of the original property (located at 67 Castle Street). This has been acknowledged through two more recent plaques that surround the Vachel inscription in its present location.

Context and Presentation

The inscription commemorating Thomas Vachel's gift of endowed almshouses teaches us another important lesson about inscriptions. Inscriptions derive their meaning not only from their words, but also the material they are written on and their environment.

The transfer of the plaque to its new location made it necessary to add an explanation to it, as the point of reference of the words 'these Alms-Houses' has changed. The removal of the plaque from its original context has rendered it an odd fix, corrupting the meaning of the inscription. Unlike literature, which can travel through time and space, inscriptions need their context as part of their meaning, and they are not so much additions to, but part of, an environment that must be interpreted.

In addition to the environment, the presentation of the inscription carries meaning as well – there are modes of communication that supplement the inscribed words.

The Latin inscription of the statue of Edward VII demonstrates this. The two long inscriptions, on either side of the pedestal, are presented as oblong plaques, with a simple frame and some minimal decoration (including Reading's shield, or *escutcheon*). The Latin inscription, however, has been inscribed in a stylised structure that resembles a winged tablet. This winged tablet, or *tabula ansata*, is both a typical shape for labels of artworks, and, more importantly, a graphic indicator of authority and rule ever since antiquity.

Radinga Latina – Latin Reading: An Anthology

Knowledge, they say, is power, and what knowledge is for the present, memory is for the past. Whoever controls what we know, holds power, and the same can be said for whoever controls or influences our memory. Whom, or what, should we remember? And why? And whom, or what, in turn, should we forget instead? Are people and things forgotten as though they never existed? Knowledge, truthful or false, that passes on from one generation to another, forms part of a tradition, a legacy, or a ritual. Only what is included in that tradition can become part of people's collective memory, and only some of that memory will become taken for granted without further inquiry or critical investigation.

The epigraphic record – the multitude of inscriptions that exist – can supplement the record of literary and oral traditions in exciting and unique ways. Looking at inscriptions, it is possible to connect immediately and directly with people, events, values, everyday and extraordinary issues of the recent and the more distant past. They preserve stories, attitudes, fates that may be completely lost otherwise. Looking at a selection that stands out even more, due to the deliberate focus on Latin inscriptions, increases and intensifies this sensation even further.

A definitive, complete selection of Latin inscriptions in Reading would easily comprise some three hundred items, from inscribed Roman clay tiles in the Reading Museum to the Abbey Seal, from Latin motto scrolls on coats of arms to monumental inscriptions on statues and buildings.

The collection in this book presents a selection of examples representing Reading as a centre of civic life and pride, a centre of commerce, a place of the cleric, of education, and as a town that was, and continues to be, home to a remarkable range of even more remarkable people. Its inscriptions give an idea of variety and change, merging tradition and individual stories and anecdotes, representative or not of the long, varied history of Reading – and the United Kingdom more generally – spanning almost 2,000 years.

In spite of its focus on a language that seems to separate the traditional and the modern, this collection aims to unify, inviting you to reconnect with Reading's past by means of translation. It brings together town and gown (both the township of Reading itself and its long-established schools and its university have a wide range of inscriptions to offer); it bridges the divide between secular and clerical Reading (Latin inscriptions can be found in Reading's churches and churchyards as well as in many other environments); and it illustrates the unbroken tradition of Latin from the ancient world to the present day, as the included inscriptions cover a timeframe of almost two thousand years.

Reading is, and long has been, a town much maligned. In recent years, Reading's failure to attract city status has once again stirred up its inhabitants' emotions. There is a common notion of twenty-first century Reading as a faceless, interchangeable commuter town in the catchment area of London. Others see Reading as one of the most exciting places due to its proximity to the UK's self-professed Silicon Valley, the gateway to the software industries in and around the town. Those perceptions, however, are regrettably narrow.

With a history of more than 1,200 years, Reading should not be reduced to a place that, once upon a time, used to have a famous abbey: the writing for Reading has been on the wall for some time – it is high time we read it.

Reading the Signs

This section provides a quick explanation, or 'key' to the symbols and methods of presentation that are used in the field of Latin epigraphy to illustrate the peculiarities of Latin texts:

abc   Regular letters, as visible in the inscription.

a(bc)   The inscription only gives the letter *a*. What is given in parenthesis has been supplied by the editor to expand an abbreviation, or expand writing that has otherwise been deliberately shortened.

[abc]   Letters that originally must have been in the inscription, but are now lost due to a mechanical disturbance of the text (e.g. physical damage).

<abc>   Letters accidentally omitted by the writer of the inscription, which were supplied by the editor in order to render the text meaningful.

`abc´   The letters enclosed by these signs, while belonging precisely where they are given in the continuous text, are written above the line of the inscription.

⌐abc⌐   The letters enclosed by half brackets replace existing letters that were engraved erroneously.

abc   Underlined letters were read by previous editors, but are now no longer visible (e.g. due to weathering of the stone).

_a|bc_   Line break between _a_ and _bc_.

_a||bc_   Change of text layout (or side of monument) between _a_ and _bc_, for example in the case of an inscription that has been arranged over multiple columns.

Latin: Language of Authority

Vergil, one of the most celebrated poets of the age of Augustus, famously wrote in the sixth book of his epic *Aeneid*:

> *tu regere imperio populos, Romane, memento,*
> *(hae tibi erunt artes), pacique imponere morem,*
> *parcere subiectis et debellare superbos.*

> 'You, Roman, remember to rule nations with your power
> (these will be your prime skills), to impose civilised behaviour upon peace,
> to spare the humbled, and to vanquish the proud in war.'

This directive, given by the mythical Anchises to his son Aeneas for his forthcoming task, the foundation of the Roman nation in Italy, enshrines an ancient Roman concept of imperialism. It also propagates and eternalises the ideology of the Romans as a people of power and rule, in war and peace.

The language of the Romans, Latin, has also often been associated with the very same ideology. Latin, in the ancient world and beyond, to the present day, is a language that has been used to communicate power and power relations, with an added sense of aristocratic dignity and tradition. It thus often features in contexts that are designed to inspire a hierarchy between the Latin speaker and those listening or reading. These associations may be little more than impressions caused by the presence of the language itself, rather than the writing's actual content or intelligibility.

The use of Latin as a prestige language, used to communicate power and might, was visible in our initial example of the statue of Edward VII. The same phenomenon forms part of everyday experience in Reading and anywhere else in the United Kingdom, if not always on a conscious level.

Latin is a constant, permanent fixture of everyday life in Britain. An obvious illustration for this would be the one pound coin: one of the various types currently in circulation comes with a Latin statement: *nemo me impune lacessit* ('no one provokes me unpunished') – a bold assertion of royal power.

A similar, if perhaps less conspicuous example can be found on virtually every post-box in the country: most post-boxes have Latin on them, in the form of the Royal cypher. Post-boxes in Britain are operated by the Royal Mail, but this is not the only reason why this graphic device has been added. Rather, the visible presence of the sovereign is a means of reinforcing existing power structures and reminding the populace of the stability and reliability that is (allegedly) guaranteed by the current constitution and government.

The following five inscriptions (1–5) are prominent examples of the presence of the Latin language in the public sphere of Reading, as expressions and assertions of power, rule, and administration.

1. Reading's Coat of Arms

Reading obtained its arms in 1566 during the reign of Elizabeth I. They were developed from a seal that can be traced back as early as the fourteenth century, but may well be older (for a version of Reading's seal see inscription 2). The arms were redeveloped into a full coat of arms in 1953, with a Latin motto added, on occasion of the coronation of Queen Elizabeth II.

An ornate painted wooden sculpture of the Reading arms is kept in the Mayor's parlour in the Civic Centre; another widely visible representation has been integrated into the south wall of Reading's Old Town Hall (facing Market Place), where it can be found in a circular structure made of red brickwork.

a.   *R(egina) E(lisabetha) (?).*

                   'Queen Elizabeth.'

b.   *A deo et regina.*

                   'From [or: by] God and the Queen.'

The central blue escutcheon, with the Queen's and the four maidens' heads as well as the letters, is supported by two rams, representing Reading's history as a centre of the wool trade, one – with a portcullis – standing for the Borough, the other – with the representation of two rivers – standing for the rivers Thames and Kennet. The shield is crowned by a knight's helmet and a mitre, the latter alluding to Reading Abbey. The mitre shows scallop shells, a symbol of the pilgrims coming to Reading, alternating with lyres, most likely to signify Reading Abbey's musical fame.

Early versions of the arms already showed the letters R and E, to the left and the right of the Queen's head. The origin and meaning of this highly unusual addition of letters as part of the central shield is unknown: it has been suggested that this may represent either the initials of the town of *Re(ading)* or denote *R(egina) E(lisabetha)*, Queen Elizabeth I. Either explanation is somewhat unsatisfactory (the former more so than the latter), and one may easily think of further alternatives, such as *R(egnante) E(lisabetha)*, 'under the reign of Elizabeth'. Some early versions (but not the earliest ones), show the letters reversed, which then could mean *E(lisabetha) R(egina)*, 'Queen Elizabeth'. None of these speculations may be accurate, and it is entirely possible that the letters go back even further, beyond the Elizabethan age. At any rate, the letters

were kept on the shield to honour Queen Elizabeth II, under whose reign the arms were redeveloped.

Whereas the central shield is visible on numerous pre-1953 structures in Reading, the full coat of arms features rather infrequently in public. The coat of arms is still in use, however, by the Mayor of Reading.

Insignia, when put on display, assert power, status, and lineage. The Latin motto of Reading's coat of arms impressively combines the common use of Latin as a prestige language in mottoes with references to powers both divine and royal.

2. Reading's Historic Seal at the Forbury Gardens Gate

This is a stylised azure shield, attached to the wings of the Victoria Gate at the south-western entrance to Forbury Gardens, commemorating Queen Victoria's Diamond Jubilee of 1897. The shield exhibits an oval seal, closely related to Reading's coat of arms (see inscription 1, above), and displays

five female heads in *saltire* (a diagonal cross formation common in heraldry), with a crowned queen's head at its centre. The surrounding frame contains a Latin inscription, with a stylised cross at the top.

S(igillum) Communitatis Radingie.

'Seal of the Community of Reading.'

The records from the 1566 visitation of Berkshire comment: 'These are the auntient [ancient] Armes and Seale apperteynynge and belonginge to the Mayor and Burgesses of the Towne and Boroughe of Readinge in the Countie of Berkes.'

The same seal, in a slightly less oval shape, can be found above the door of Blake's Lock Sewage Pumping Station.

3. A Statue of Queen Victoria

A statue of Queen Victoria stands opposite the main entrance of St Laurence's church, facing north. The marble-clad pedestal is inscribed at the front (in a decorative shield) and at the rear. The main (front) inscription is in Latin; a second inscription, at the rear of the pedestal, is in English and explains the occasion.

Victoria
D(ei) g(ratia)
Britanniar(um) reg(ina)
Indiae imp(eratrix)
fid(ei) def(ensor).
MDCCC
LXXX
VII.

'Victoria,
by grace of God,
queen of the Britains,
empress of India,
defender of the faith.
1887.'

The statue was erected in 1887, the year in which Queen Victoria's golden jubilee was celebrated on 20 and 21 June. It was produced by George Blackall Simonds, who was

VICTORIA
D: G:
BRITANNIAR: REG:
INDIÆ IMP:
FID: DEF:
MDCCC
LXXX
VII

also responsible for the lion in Reading's Forbury Gardens. As the statue faces away from the town centre, it sparked the (unsubstantiated) myth that Queen Victoria was not particularly fond of Reading and thus chose not to face it.

As in the case of her son Edward (p. 1–4), Latin is used for the official titulature of the monarch. Due to its length and presentation, it makes a powerful statement in a public space, a statement of power, asserting the status quo, and visualising the distance between the onlookers and the honorand.

Unlike in the case of King Edward – where this impression is mitigated by the existence of substantial inscriptions in English, and with prominent mention of people other than the honorand – the statue of Queen Victoria, with its inscription, is presented in a significantly more distanced and cold way than that of her son.

A little-noticed English inscription on this statue can be seen on the rear of the pedestal. Even though the letters are quite large, the lack of contrast, partly caused by the fact that the letters are not engraved very deeply into the surface, makes it very hard to read (and to spot):

Erected
to commemorate
the completion of
the fiftieth year of
Her Majesty's reign,
June 20th, 1887.
Arthur Hill, Mayor.

The direct comparison with the statue of Edward VII highlights the matter-of-fact brevity of this text and its focus on factual information. Mention of the Mayor's name lends an official signature to this statue, thus rendering this landmark a record of civic obedience in the public sphere, presented in modest distance to the powerful presence of Her Majesty the Queen and her Latin titulature.

The most intriguing aspect of the Latin inscription on the front is perhaps the phrase *Britanniarum Regina*, 'Queen of the Britains'. It was not until the mid-nineteenth century that the originally imperialist notion of a 'Greater Britain' was actively promoted. It became a political catchphrase following the publication of Sir Charles Dilke's 1868 work *Greater Britain: A Record of Travel in English-Speaking Countries During* 1866 *and* 1867. The plural 'Britains' here refers to the United Kingdom in its entirety, the British kingdoms as well as its colonies. Special mention is made of India, where Victoria also held the title of Empress.

4. A Statue of Lord Rufus Isaacs

This marble statue is located at the southern end of the King George V Gardens, Eldon Square, off London Road. It commemorates Rufus Isaacs, 1st Marquess of Reading (1860–1935) and Viceroy of India (1920–26).

Lord Isaacs was not only connected with Reading by name, but he also resided in Foxhill House, a listed building on the Whiteknights estate, currently home to the University's Law School. His statue, produced by Charles Sargeant Jagger, one of Britain's best-known war memorial artists, was originally set up in Delhi to commemorate Lord Isaacs's Viceroyship. (Note that the statue does not carry an inscription that identifies the honorand by name.) It was transferred to Reading in the late 1960s, and it was unveiled in 1971 in its present location.

a.

Aut nunquam tentes, aut per 'f'ice'!'

'Either do not attempt at all, or do it perfectly.'

b.

C(harles) S(argeant) Jagger
Sc(ulpsit).

'C. S. Jagger sculpted (this).'

Text *a*, as given above, is different from what is clearly written on the stone: instead of the final *perfice!*, the sculptor has written *PERSICEI*. The motto's first half, *aut nunquam tentes*, in perfectly good Latin, means as much as 'either do not attempt at all'. The second half, however, in its inscribed form *persicei* means ... absolutely nothing! While this may be partly down to the fact that Latin rarely makes much sense to those who come into contact with it – even more true for many Latin mottoes – the error is due to a rather outstanding mistake by the sculptor. What he *should* have written was *aut perfice!* (with an exclamation mark), meaning 'or do it perfectly!'

How could he have got such an important detail wrong? The explanation for this must be in the model upon which Jagger had based the execution of the coat of arms. In 1930s handwriting, for example, or in several typefaces of the time, the letters F and S, in their lower-case forms, would have been almost indistinguishable, the only difference being a minuscule horizontal line.

The sculptor (or the person who modelled the coat of arms for him) must have misread, and then created this howler when transcribing the text into capital letters. This is also where an original exclamation mark at the end of the motto appears to have turned into the final *-i* of the meaningless word *persicei*. A blunder in the Latin term for 'do it perfectly', of course, is rather ironic.

5. Arms of Thames Valley Police

One of the main tasks of any functioning state is to ensure the health and well-being of its citizens. One means of this is the provision of a functioning law enforcement agency, commonly referred to as the police. For Reading, the relevant police force is Thames Valley Police (formerly known as Thames Valley Constabulary), responsible for Oxfordshire, Buckinghamshire and Berkshire. Thames Valley Police uses its coat of arms as part of its visual identity in the public domain, and it features prominently, for example, above the entrance to the Reading Police Station in Castle Street.

Armorial bearings were granted in 1971 when the Thames Valley Constabulary was given permission to rename itself as Thames Valley Police. The central piece of the arms is a shield with a river and five crowns, representing the river Thames and the five police forces that were merged into the Thames Valley Constabulary in 1968. Below the shield there is a scroll that contains the Latinised motto of Thames Valley Police:

Sit pax in valle Tamesis.

'Let there be peace in the Thames Valley.'

As is common in mottoes, the aspirational claim, stating the motivation for Thames Valley Police, is in Latin, traditionally used as a prestige language in such contexts.

The use of the Latin word *pax*, 'peace' is interesting, as it is somewhat at odds with its use in antiquity; the Latin word *pax* does not typically denote an effect of 'peace' (such as 'peaceful state', 'order', or 'prosperity'), but its conditions – a behaviour regulated through the existence of a treaty, a firm, often documented relationship between various groups of people.

Very much like its English translation 'peace', one hears *bellum*, 'war', as the opposite – but the prevention of war (or civil war) through treaty is not within the remit of Thames Valley Police. So we may wonder why the notion of *pax* was adopted for this motto of a law enforcement agency rather than, say, *concordia* ('harmony') or *iustitia* ('justice').

Church Latin

In the first section we looked at examples for the use of Latin as a language of prestige and power, in the context of rule and administration. The contrast between Latin as a language that is not commonly used or understood on the one hand, and its continued presence in contexts in which power and control are asserted on the other, highlights how language can be deliberately used to communicate and consolidate social structures.

This section presents examples of the use of Latin in the context of the Christian Church in Reading. The Western Christian tradition originates from and is deeply rooted in the tradition of the Roman Church, in which Latin continues to play an important role. This tradition manifests itself in the frequent use of Latin in inscriptions that relate to issues of Christian worship and belief.

It would be wrong to claim that Latin in Christian contexts has not been used as a tool to exercise power and control: quite the contrary! It is not possible to over-emphasise the liberating aspect of bible translations, especially from the time of the Reformation onwards, allowing those unable to read Latin to access scripture in their own languages. Nevertheless, Latin continues to play a prominent role in the Christian Church, in a virtually unbroken tradition from antiquity, and in this context its role is substantially different from that of Latin used in other contexts.

The following ten examples (6–15) give a selective overview of the wealth of Latin inscriptions that can be found in Reading churches, and cover the wide range of different types and materials that one may encounter. (See also 32, 36, and 47 for related inscriptions in other categories.) It is not surprising that the inscriptions in this category often contain quotations of, or allusions to, Christian texts from the Bible and from hymns in particular.

In many cases, the inscription thus becomes almost a decorative feature of a cult object rather than a piece of actual written communication with an audience.

6. The High Altar of Reading Minster

The Reading Minster of St Mary the Virgin can pride itself on its ornate and richly decorated screen or *reredos* on the High Altar. It is a lavish piece made of gilded oak, dating to the mid-1930s. Representations of winged angels surround the central crucifixion scene and an inscription runs along the top edge. The text is interrupted by the arched crucifixion scene:

Adoramus te Christe et benedicimus tibi
'We adore Thee, o Christ, and we bless Thee ...'

ADORAMVS TE CHRISTE ET BENEDICIMVS TIBI

QVIA PER CRVCEM TVAM REDEMISTI MVNDVM

quia per crucem tuam redemisti mundum
'... who by Thy Cross hath redeemed the world.'

This is a version of part of a stanza 'Adoramus te', traditionally recited during the Stations of the Cross. Incidentally, the original version of the text has an additional word that is lacking on Reading's altar: it reads *per <sanctam> crucem tuam* ('by Thy <Holy> Cross').

7. Inscribed Sundial of St Laurence's Church

This is an eighteenth-century rectangular sundial mounted to the south wall of the bell tower of St Laurence's church. It is made of sandstone with a metal gnomon.

The sundial indicates the hours of the day with lines and Arabic numerals carved into the stone. It also notes the year 1727 and contains the letters *G* and *P*, perhaps referring to George Paine (or Payn), churchwarden at the time. At the top end of the sundial, there is a Latin inscription:

Vigilate et orate.

'Watch and pray.'

This is a reference to the New Testament, Matthew 26:41, where Jesus admonishes Peter, as the disciples had fallen asleep in Gethsemane: 'So, could you not watch with me one hour? Watch and pray that you may not enter into temptation. The spirit indeed is willing, but the flesh is weak.'

8. Painted Ceiling in the Chancel of St Laurence's

This painted wooden ceiling above the chancel of St Laurence's is inscribed on its northern and southern sides in black letters with red ornaments. While the chancel dates to the earliest (medieval) phase of the church, its ceiling with its current decoration in red, white, and black and its Christogram (IHS) would appear to date to 1847.

The painted text is broken down into 14 segments, seven on the northern side and seven on the southern. The final two segments (running from north to south) at the east end of the chancel have an additional set of one-word inscriptions painted on them (*laus, postestas, honor, gloria* – 'praise, might, honour, glory').

a. North side of the chancel

+ Cum | Angelis et | Archangelis cumque | omni Militia | Caelestis exercitus | gloriosom Nomen | tuum laudamus ||,

'With Angels and Archangels and with all the hosts of the heavenly army, we laud thy glorious Name,'

b. South side of the Chancel

et magnificamus. | Te sine fine | celebrantes ac dicentes: | Sanctus, Sanctus | Sanctus | Dominus Deus | Sabaoth: Amen.

'and magnify it. We evermore praise you and say: Holy, holy, holy, Lord God of Sabaoth [*i.e.* 'of hosts']: Amen.'

The inscription gives a version of the concluding words of the Proper Preface of the Eucharistic Prayer (or Holy Communion) – an important part of the traditional Order of Mass, a Christian sacrament that re-enacts the Last Supper, as represented in the New Testament.

The sixth segment of the text written on the north side of the ceiling has a peculiar misspelling in the word *gloriosom* ('glorious'), which should read *gloriosum*.

9. Painted Ceiling in the Chancel of St Giles-in-Reading

The ceiling of the chancel of St Giles-in-Reading, dating to Victorian times, is sustained by a complex structure of wooden beams strikingly painted in bright red, with decorative elements in white and black. The beams that form the lower border of this structure exhibit a painted inscription, in black Gothic script on white ground, which starts at the northern side of the chancel and runs towards the stained glass window at the eastern end and continues on the southern side.

The text is broken into ten parts, segmented by the complex wooden framework. There are many abbreviations and contractions in the Latin words. The letterforms are close to that of a book typeface (but note the curved initial B!), whereas the representation of abbreviations and contractions is reminiscent of Latin manuscripts and early prints.

a. North side of the chancel

Beatus vir q(ui) timet d(omin)um, || i(n) ma(n)datis ej(us) volet nimis. || potens i(n) terra erit semen, || generatio rectoru(m) benedicetur. || gloria et divitiae i(n) domo ej(us),

b. South side of the chancel

justitia ej(us) manet i(n) saec(u)l(um) saec(u)li. || i(n) memoria aeterna erit justus || ab auditione mala non timebit. || dispersit dedit pauperibu(s); || justitia ej(us) manet i(n) saec(u)l(um) saec(u)li.

The text offers phrases from Psalm 112 (Psalm 111 of the Greek and the Latin Vulgate). The first six segments (the whole text of the northern part of the inscription as well as the first segment of the southern part) are phrases 1–3, with the omission of an *et*, ('and') at the beginning of segment 6. The remaining four segments provide a mixture of phrases 6, 7, and 9 of the psalm, which, in full, reads as follows. The phrases covered by the inscription are underlined:

1 Blessed is the man who fears the Lord,
  who greatly delights in his commandments!
2 His offspring will be mighty in the land;
  the generation of the upright will be blessed.
3 Wealth and riches are in his house,
  and his righteousness endures forever.
4 Light dawns in the darkness for the upright;
  he is gracious, merciful, and righteous.
5 It is well with the man who deals generously and lends;
  who conducts his affairs with justice.
6 For the righteous will never be moved;
  he will be remembered forever.
7 He is not afraid of bad news;
  his heart is firm, trusting in the Lord.
8 His heart is steady; he will not be afraid,
  until he looks in triumph on his adversaries.
9 He has distributed freely; he has given to the poor;
  his righteousness endures forever;
  his horn is exalted in honour.
10 The wicked man sees it and is angry;
  he gnashes his teeth and melts away;
  the desire of the wicked will perish!

10. Decorated Arch of Our Lady and St Anne's Church

This monument with sculpture and inscription is inserted in the brick wall above the main (west) entrance to Our Lady and St Anne's church, Caversham (built 1902–21).

a. In a scroll

Is(aiah) XI.I.

b. At the bottom

Egredietur virga de radice Jesse. || Is(aiah) | XI.

'There shall come forth a shoot from the stump of Jesse. (Is. 11:1)'

The so-called Tree of Jesse has been a popular motif in Christian iconography from the Middle Ages. Jesse was the father of the biblical King David, and the Book of Isaiah, at the relevant passage, describes the descent of a Messiah – a passage that in the Christian tradition has been read as a prophecy related to Jesus Christ (Is. 11:1–5):

'There shall come forth a shoot from the stump of Jesse,
and a branch from his roots shall bear fruit.
And the Spirit of the Lord shall rest upon him,
the Spirit of wisdom and understanding,

the Spirit of counsel and might,
the Spirit of knowledge and the fear of the Lord.
And his delight shall be in the fear of the Lord.
He shall not judge by what his eyes see,
or decide disputes by what his ears hear,
but with righteousness he shall judge the poor,
and decide with equity for the meek of the earth;
and he shall strike the earth with the rod of his mouth,
and with the breath of his lips he shall kill the wicked.
Righteousness shall be the belt of his waist,
and faithfulness the belt of his loins.'

11. Funerary Monument for John Canon Ringrose

In the north-western corner of St James's churchyard, adjacent to the forecourt of Reading Gaol, there is a small collection of headstones and funerary monuments. Originally the churchyard extended further to the north, a space now taken up by Forbury Road. Closer to the church building itself, there is a humble, now damaged, monument made of red granite that displays a Latin inscription.

Orate pro anima
Adm(odum) R(everen)d(i) Joannis Canonici Ringrose
primi hujus ecc(lesi)ae
annos XXXIV rectoris qui pie in d(omi)no obdormivit
XXVIII Oct(obris) MDCCCLXXIV aet(atis) LXX.
Benemerenti amici merentes posuere.

'Pray for the soul
of the Very Rev'd. John Canon Ringrose,
the first rector of this church
for 34 years, who, piously, fell asleep in the Lord
on the 28th of October 1874, aged 70.
Deserving friends erected this to him who was well deserving.'

St James's is a Roman Catholic church designed in a Norman Romanesque style by A. W. N. Pugin and built on the ruins of Reading Abbey in 1840. The driving force behind this, the first Catholic church built in Reading since the Reformation (and incidentally Pugin's first attempt at a church building), was James Wheble, who had commissioned the building from Pugin in 1837.

The Very Rev'd. John Canon Ringrose, commemorated by this funerary inscription, was the church's first rector.

12. Inscribed Tile for M. J. G. Melrose

This engraved floor tile is inserted into the floor of the north transept of St Giles-in-Reading church, at the bottom of the steps of the Altar of the Holy Souls.

Michael James Gervase | Melrose | 17.12.1947 –19.7.2009 |
Rector and Vicar | MCMXCIV – MMIX.

Anima eius et animae omnium fidelium | per misericordiam
Dei requiescant in pace.

'May his soul and the souls of all faithful men rest in peace
through the mercifulness of God.'

Father Michael Melrose had been parish priest of the Anglo-Catholic church of St Giles-in-Reading for fifteen years, when he suddenly died of a stroke in 2009. Born in Edinburgh, he studied at the University of Durham and was ordained as a priest in 1971.

Described in obituaries as a 'very wise priest and a very gentle priest' who 'had a love for art, literature, and architecture', Melrose was a staunch supporter of Latin. The Latin phrase on the tile is a reminder of that.

13. Inscribed Altar in Holy Trinity Church

This lavishly decorated altar at the south-west end of the main nave of the Church of the Most Holy Trinity, Oxford Road, has an inscribed reredos.

Fructus ejus dulcis gutturi meo.

'His fruit (was) sweet to my taste.'

This is a quote from the Song of Solomon (2:3), from a passage that reads as follows:

> 'As an apple tree among the trees of the forest,
> so is my beloved among the young men.
> With great delight I sat in his shadow,
> and his fruit was sweet to my taste.'

Presumably thought to be understood metaphorically by the person who commissioned this piece, this turns into a remarkably daring (nay, fruity) motto for an altar piece, once the context is taken into account.

14. The Yates Windows of Reading Minster

A stained glass window, at the east end in the north wall of the north aisle of Reading Minster, bears this inscription:

In honorem dei et memoriam C(harlotte) A(nne) Yates || matris piae et desideratae hanc fenestram || quatuor filiae grato animo dedicaverunt. Obiit || April 4th A(nno) D(omini) 1839, Aetatis suae 44. Requiescam i<n> pace.

> 'In honour of god and to the memory of C. A. Yates, their pious and beloved mother, her four daughters dedicated this window, gratefully. She died on 4th of April, AD 1839, aged 44. May I rest in peace.'

Charlotte Anne Yates (née Peel) was born in 1795 and was married to Rev. Samuel Wildman Yates, MA (1793–1862), who was the vicar at Reading Minster for 25 years. Charlotte Anne – like her husband of noble descent – died young, but had children. The names of two daughters are easily established through marriage registers – Elizabeth Harriott Fitzgerald (née Yates), and Susannah Louisa Georgina Francis (née Yates).

In Honorem Dei et memoriam C A Yate
natu... filia beatæ an... dedicaverunt On...

...atris b... et De...dere fecit hanc fenestram
Anno A D 1839 Ætatis... 844 Renui... ram Walt...

The Latin is not free from oddities. Note in particular the insertion of the English date 'April 4th' instead of the Latinised form '4° Apr(ilis)' or similar, and the strange shift from the third person to the first person singular in the valedictory phrase *Requiescam in pace*, 'May I rest in peace' (as opposed to *Requiescat in pace*, 'May she rest in peace'). The letter *-n* of *in* has also been omitted.

Dubious Latin skills can be found in another stained glass window in Reading Minster, and again this is related to the Yates family. This window, largely destroyed during the Second World War, is to the south of the Lady Chapel. Only the three smaller top windows survive, and the inscription in question is in the top window, below the coat of arms of the Yates family:

> *Per rege et patria.*

The motto of the Yates, as part of their coat of arms, is *pro rege et patria*, 'for God and country'. This has been corrupted here, replacing the Latin preposition *pro* ('for') with *per* ('by means of'), rendering the motto meaningless and ungrammatical.

15. Our Lady of Walsingham Plaque (St Giles-in-Reading)

This coloured plaque is attached to the south wall of St Giles's Lady Chapel. The circular plaque depicts Mary and Jesus according to the 'Our Lady of Walsingham' iconography: Mary is seated, as a queen, on a throne, with Jesus in her lap. The image is surrounded by a framed margin that displays the inscription, with a Christian cross symbol at the top, to mark the beginning and ending of the words.

Ave Maria, gratia <pl>ena, dominus tecum.

'Hail Mary, full of grace. Our Lord is with thee.'

The inscription gives the first six words of the famous *Ave Maria* ('Hail Mary') hymn. Notice that the first two letters of the word *plena* ('full') are missing. Due to a possible planning mishap in the arrangement of the text, those two letters seem to be hiding behind the left leg of Mary's throne.

Latin Business

How do the Latin language and the world of business go together? In a world where trade and business appear to be ever accelerating, it seems counter-intuitive that a language often perceived as elitist, inaccessible and not consumer-friendly does in fact have its place.

The following six inscriptions (16–21) give an overview of the uses of Latin in the world of trade – from its original context on a Roman clay lamp (16) to its manifestations in shop signs of recent times. This is supplemented by a funerary inscription (17) in which an eighteenth-century businessman from Bristol commemorates and idealises his Reading-born wife, a remarkable expression of the values and aspirations of these people at that time. One could supplement this section further with inscriptions that celebrate local benefactors (40), craftsmen (42), and the like in other contexts.

What all of these texts have in common, with the exception of the funerary inscription, is their desire for pithy expressions of great brevity. Latin lends itself to this with great ease, with the additional benefit of a connotation of prestige and style (if not class). In that regard, the most common use of Latin in the world of business is in the context of motto phrases, as part of armorial achievements, authentic or imagined. When displayed, they help to convey impressions of grandeur and legacy.

Brevity and the use of (often widely known or easily explicable) stock phrases help to enable understanding across the language divide. This example is published in a 'Book of Words' of a Reading Historical Pageant (1920), illustrating the development of Sutton's Seeds, who were then still based at Market Place:

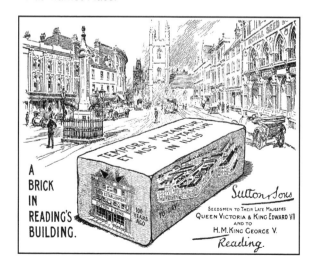

The 'Brick in Reading's Building' is inscribed *tempora mutantur, et nos mutamur in illis* ('times change, and we change with them') – a famous adage, perhaps inspired by Heraclitus' concept of *panta rhei* ('everything is in flux'), but also resembling a line in Ovid's *Metamorphoses*. Little knowledge of Latin was needed to unlock this line's meaning – those who did not know this memorable sentiment in the original could just look it up in a book of famous phrases and sayings.

Finally, Latin has, and continues to have, its place in makers' marks. In a long tradition throughout European craftsmanship and art history (at least in certain professions), the producers of paintings, sculpture, and technical objects (including bells) sign their work in Latin. Several examples of this practice can be found in Reading – see the Roman clay lamp (16) and also, for example, the statue of Lord Rufus Isaacs (4b).

16. A Roman Clay Lamp

This simple, undecorated terracotta lamp of Roman origin is mould-made and conforms to a common type of Roman clay lamps. It has a circular, bowl-shaped body, a rounded shoulder, a small flat discus on the top with a raised rim, and a nozzle which is connected to the discus with a channel. There are three lugs on the lamp's shoulder.

The lamp is on display in the Ure Museum of Greek Archaeology at the Department of Classics at the University of Reading (Whiteknights Campus, Humanities and Social Sciences Building). The exact findspot is unknown. The bottom of the lamp reveals a moulded inscription in Latin letters.

Vibiani.
'Vibianus™'

Vibianus was a household name in the Roman lamp market of the second century AD. The name indicates the producer, Vibianus, who was a businessman and the owner of one of most successful lamp-producing businesses in the Roman Empire. His lamps were mass-produced in proto-industrial factories and workshops for a mass market. He started his business in the second century AD, presumably in Northern Italy, and it expanded rapidly, with branch offices at the market alongside the Danube (e.g. at Regensburg/Ratisbon), and perhaps pushing competitors out of their businesses by the end of the century.

There is evidence that Vibianus' trademark was in fact so successful that others were producing unauthorised versions of his product, to cash in on the successful brand he had established.

The presence of the name Vibianus on these lamps may be seen as a trademark, a seal guaranteeing a certain standard and quality. Equally, it can be seen as an inscription that served a more practical need: the need to identify one's lot in a kiln that produced lamps for more than one workshop, and the need to organise the logistics of commerce when feeding these lamps into the market.

17. Funerary Inscription for Cordelia Hollidge (née Terrel)

This sizeable marble monument is attached to the south wall of the main nave of St Giles-in-Reading.

H(ic) s(ubter) j(acet)
Cordelia,
Johannis Hollidge, de Bristolis Mercatoris
Uxor:
Thomae & Eleanorae Terrel de Reading Filia:
Quae obiit 21o Martii 1723
Aetatis 21o.
Virtutes Sociales Domesticis ijs decoravit
quae Mulierem vel commendant vel faciunt;
Nec minus Intemerati in Deum Animi
Eximia edidit Specimina
Vitamq(ue) Brevem heu & Perangustam nimis
Sed Innocuam vixit & Suis Iucundam.
Ideoq(ue) tantum vixit
Ut Maestius, ut Diuturnius Sui relinqueret Desiderium,
Ni forsan & Tu, Lector, imitando effeceris
Ut Ea minus desideretur.
In perpetuum intimi Amoris Monumentum
Conjux Maestissimus
Hoc Marmor poni voluit.

'Here below lies
Cordelia, wife of John Hollidge, a merchant from Bristol,
daughter of Thomas and Eleanor Terrel of Reading,
who died 21st of March, 1723, aged 21.
Her social virtues she adorned with those domestic ones
that commend a wife – or make one;
to no lesser extent she gave outstanding examples
of a steadfast spirit towards God.
She lived a life short, alas, and all too constrained,
but free from harm and delightful for her relatives.

H . S . J.

Cordelia,
Johannis Holledge, de Brithdir Mercatoris
Uxor:
Thomæ & Eleanoræ Terrel de Reading Filia
Quæ obiit 21.º Martij 1722.
Ætatis 16.

Virtutes Sociales Domesticas iis decoravit,
Quæ Mulierem vel commendant vel faciunt,
Nec minus Ingenuitate in Deum Anima
Eximia edidit Specimina:
Vitamq, Brevem heu! & Peractogratam nimis
Sed Innocuam vixit & Suis Jucundam,
Ideoq, tantum vixit
Ut Mæstius, ut Diuturnius Sui relinqueret Desiderium
Ni forsan & Tu, Lector imitando effeceris
Ut Ea minus desideretur.

In perpetuum intimi Amoris Monimentum,
Conjux Mæstissimus
Hoc Marmor poni voluit.

Thus she lived but to leave behind a desire of herself
so very saddening, so very lasting
– unless you, Reader, perchance, will succeed and come close to her,
so that she will be missed less at last.
Her most heartbroken husband wanted this stone to be set
as an eternal monument to intimate love.'

The Terrel(l)s – Thomas and Eleanor – are listed as the parents of numerous children, Mary (born in 1686), Robert (1687), Eleanor (1688), Elizabeth (1690), and a late arrival, Cordelia (1702). Cordelia married John Hollidge, a merchant from Bristol, as the inscription states. Several of his activities in Bristol in the first half of the eighteenth century are documented in surviving records, including one that mentions bankruptcy of a Bristol merchant named John Hollidge on 1 March 1736.

The wording of this eighteenth-century piece, while intimate and an expression of deep love and grief, conveys a view of 'the ideal woman' that is strikingly out of date, or so one would hope, some three hundred years later. It is also a fine example of a monument that sings the praises of the deceased without any mention of specific achievements; which social virtues, and which domestic ones, did Cordelia actually display – and which ones 'make' a wife (at least in the eyes of an eighteenth-century merchant)?

The inscription's final movement, exhorting its readership to live up to the example of virtuousness set by Cordelia, renders a common expression of this genre (see also inscriptions 40 and 47) rather heavy-handed.

18. The *Reading Mercury*

This Latin motto, on a motto scroll, is part of an armorial achievement placed at the top of an advertising banner for a now defunct Reading newspaper, the *Reading Mercury*. The banner dates to approximately 1900.

The graphic device combines elements of the United Kingdom's coat of arms (the lion and the unicorn, facing outwards rather than inwards, a modification of the UK's coat of arms) and Reading's own arms (the blue shield at the centre).

Floreat Readingensis.

'May the Readingite flourish.'

The *Reading Mercury* started its life in 1723 and eventually became a comparatively political and liberal outlet in the first half of the

nineteenth century, reflecting the overall change in mentality at that time.

The Latin motto used here, usually in the variant spelling *Floreat Redingensis*, conforms to that of Reading School (for which it has been explained as 'May Reading School flourish').

The paper was run for almost 130 years by the Cowslade family, who maintained close (at least professional and commercial) links to the Valpy family, notably Abraham John Valpy and his father Richard Valpy, master of Reading School, who is mentioned in inscription 25 below.

19. Arms of Midland Bank

A sculpture of the arms of the now defunct Midland Bank is attached to the facade of 26–28 Broad Street, currently occupied by a branch of HSBC. The inscription reads:

Vis unita fortior.

'A force united is stronger.'

Older residents of Reading may still remember that the building now occupied by HSBC once was the location of the Midland Bank. This bank was founded in 1836, acquired by HSBC in 1992, and rebranded in 1999.

The central shield, surrounded by floral patterns, represents a version of the coat of arms of the City of Birmingham. The Latin motto (that of Stoke-on-Trent) was part of the coat of arms description, or *blazon,* granted to Midland Bank officially in 1952. However, both the motto and the shield, in variations, were in use much earlier for the same company.

In a time that has seen considerable upheaval and unrest in the globalised financial markets, it is beautifully ironic that the Latin inscription and the crest are the only part of the Midland Bank that has survived – a bank swallowed by HSBC, now hijacking Midland's Latin motto as well, a motto that seems to suggest that, even for banks, joining forces is the sole hope for survival.

20. The Wynford Arms

This painted motto forms part of an armorial achievement displayed on the sign of the Wynford Arms pub on Kings Road. The central shield is divided into four equal parts, with each side showing one field with an azure fleur-de-lis and one with a vertical chevron. The scroll that runs below the shield is inscribed with a Latin motto. Neither the arms on display, nor their motto phrase, are those of the Barons Wynford.

Videre non est credere.

'To see is not to believe.'

It may be possible to trace the motto's roots to John 6:30: 'So they said to him, "Then what sign do you do, that we may see and believe you?"' or to John 20:29: 'Jesus said to him [St Thomas], "Have you believed because you have seen me? Blessed are those who have not seen and yet have believed."' In that regard, the motto suggests that faith, or belief, does not require visual (or any other form of concrete) evidence.

This explanation may be turned on its head, however, by the German mathematician Georg Cantor, who, in his correspondence with Richard Dedekind, expressed his disbelief: 'Je le vois, mais je ne le crois pas!' ('I see that, but I do not believe it.') Here, in contrast to the Christian interpretation, belief is absent, in spite of the clear, manifest evidence. The Latin sentence, very much like its English translation, is open to either interpretation.

21. The Restoration

The street sign of The Restoration pub at 928 Oxford Road, (known as The Bell until the late 1980s), bears a Latin motto inscribed on a scroll. The inscription runs through a multi-layered image, which is designed as a blend of a coat of arms and the depiction of a bricklayer.

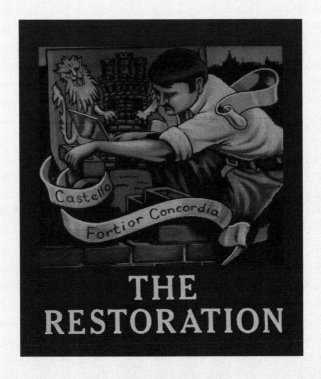

Castello fortior concordia.

'Concord is stronger than a fortress.'

The motto *Castello fortior concordia* is that of the city of Northampton, whose coat of arms is part of the iconography in the sign (partly covered by the bricklayer – the latter possibly an allusion to the nearby brickworks).

The invocation of concord on the sign appears to have made little impression on the patrons: many a brawl was reported from this now closed public house.

Learned Reading

Reading has long been established as a centre of scholarship in the arts and humanities as well as in science. Reading Abbey attracted scholarly and artistic souls, whose work and learning is still visible in the manuscripts that survived the Abbey itself. Reading is home to several highly prestigious schools – many of them not only at the top of national league tables, but priding themselves on their history and tradition as well as an impressive list of famous alumni and alumnae.

This important element of the town's history was furthered by the establishment of what was eventually to become the University of Reading. The roots of the university go back to the mid-nineteenth century, when University College, Reading, was founded, originally as an extension to Christ Church College, Oxford. This institution eventually became one the main constituents of the University of Reading, which received its Royal Charter in 1926.

Reading has also been home to a great number of learned individuals – scholars and scientists, teachers, clergymen, professionals and amateurs who held a deep interest in the world of learning and science. (See also the now lost inscription 52.)

The question of whether advanced teaching of Latin literature took place in Reading and its immediate vicinity from as early as the Roman period is open to debate: one puzzling piece of evidence, presumably from nearby Silchester, has been included to give an idea of just how long this tradition may have been (22).

Individuals and institutions alike have left their traces in the inscribed record of Reading. Many of them have chosen to do so in Latin, and many of them have rather more to contribute than just the odd remark designed to impress. Unlike many of the earlier examples, they rarely used Latin merely as an expression of privilege, power, and status. Instead, they have done so as an expression of their learnedness, using the traditional lingua franca of scholarship (and the church) of previous times.

22. Vergil in Silchester

This Roman hollow tile (*tubulus*), made of red clay, was inscribed with a sharp object before being baked. Reportedly found in Silchester, neither its provenance nor the exact circumstances of its discovery can be established with certainty. The letterforms are typical of Roman handwriting and give the impression of an experienced, if somewhat careless, writer. The object, which appears to date to the second century or slightly later, is in Reading Museum (REDMG 1995.1.26) and is currently on display in the Silchester Gallery.

Pertacus, Perfidus,
Campester, Lucilianus,
Campanus: conticuere omnes.

'Pertacus, Perfidus, Campester, Lucilianus,
Campanus: they all fell silent.'

The inscription begins with a list of Roman names (although *Perfidus* is not commonly used as a personal name, simply meaning 'perfidious'), followed by the words *conticuere omnes*, 'they all fell silent'. While this may seem like a curse-like statement at first (and it may be just that!), it has triggered significant academic interest, as these are the opening words of the second book of the *Aeneid*, an epic poem written by the Roman author Vergil – words that often appear as a quote in ancient Roman inscriptions.

Vergil, a poet from the period of Emperor Augustus, was one of the most well-known authors of Roman antiquity, and quotes of his lines, especially in casual writing, tended to be used as 'school exercises'. The fluent handwriting of this piece, however, combined with its curse-like context, suggests otherwise: this was not written by a schoolboy, but was deliberately – while borrowing Vergil's famous words – written onto a tile that was to be integrated into a built structure, so that the writer's disdain for the named individuals would become monumental and permanent.

23. Mottoes of Reading Schools

Many Reading-based schools have mottoes, commonly in Latin. Not all of them, however, have them on display in an inscribed form. The following two examples are easily accessible – one from Abbey School (inscribed repeatedly, e.g. at the gates of Abbey Junior School on Christchurch Road), and one from St Joseph's College (again inscribed repeatedly, e.g. as part of the logo on a school sign at Upper Redlands Road and Alexandra Road).

a. Motto of Abbey School

In aedificationem corporis Christi.

'For the edifying of the body of Christ.'

b. Motto of St Joseph's College

Optima deo.

'(My) best for God.'

The motto of Abbey School is derived from Ephesians 4:12:

'to equip the saints for the work of ministry, for building up the body of Christ'

Motto phrases are, or were, designed to give direction and purpose to the students' achievements as well as to the teachers' educational style, and also, certainly in the case of Latin mottoes, to aggrandise the schools' reputation. For a particularly noteworthy example, see inscription 24.

To illustrate the extent to which motto phrases can be part of everyday practice and behaviour, St Joseph's College's own promotional materials state that 'Pupils should write Optima Deo at the start of every piece of work they do at St Joseph's. This helps them remember that each piece of work should be your best.'

24. The Latin Motto of Phoenix College

A blue sign for Phoenix College, placed at the bottom of the school's front car park, facing Christchurch Road, informs passers-by about the school's name, contact details, and management. The top part of the sign lists the school's name ('Phoenix College'), with a red stylised bird and a motto written in yellow lower-case letters above.

Ad astra per aspira.

'To the stars through ... aspire!'

According to the college's website, '*Ad Astra Per Aspira* in Latin means to aspire for the stars. Our school endeavours to help students reach up to their potential.'

Schools and other educational institutions would not commonly use a Latin motto phrase expressing ambition and attitude, which is why this one is kept separate from examples 23a–b. This remarkable sentiment, as it stands written on this sign, is composed in nonsensical Latin – the Latin simply does not say what those who composed it thought it did. It is an imaginative corruption of the well-known Latin motto *Per aspera ad astra*, 'through hardship to the stars'. The Latin for 'hardship' (literally 'hard things'), *aspera*, in its common English pronunciation sounds just about close enough to *aspira* – so why not go all the way and change the spelling, to produce the aspirational claim?

It is easy enough to find mistakes in Latin texts, as we can see from other examples in this collection. For those who run Phoenix College, however, a school providing an education for boys who have emotional, behavioural and social disorders, to have (unknowingly, no doubt) turned the *aspera*, the hardships, into *aspira*, a claim for aspirations, seems beautifully appropriate and commendable; one has to approve the result, however grammatically questionable it may be.

25. Monument for Richard Valpy

This monument commemorating Richard Valpy is in St Laurence's church, worked into the north-east-facing outer wall of the tower stairwell of the nave, adjacent to the font. In its current presentation, the entire monument consists of a statue, a commemorative inscription, and an inscribed doorframe.

M(emoriae) S(acrum).
Ricardi Valpy S(anctae) T(heologiae) P(rofessor)
qui
Scholae Readingensi
annos L amplius praefuit,
summa ingenii doctrinae benevolentiae laude floruit,
singularem famae celebritatem
scriptis et docendi peritia assecutus est,
discipulos maxima frequentia huc convenientes
ad humanitatem, virtutem, pietatem
cura et praeceptis fideliter informavit,
optimarum ipse artium et virtutum omnium
exemplar simul et magister.
Hoc qualecunque monimentum
praeceptoris sui quasi sancti parentis
grate memores
nonulli ex alumnis
p(oni) (curaverunt).

In Christo decessit
Londini
V Kal(endas) Apr(iles) A(nno) D(omini) MDCCCXXXVI, aetatis LXXXI,
et in coemeterio suburbano
iuxta viam Harroviensem
sepultus est.

'Dedicated to the Memory of Richard Valpy, Doctor of Divinity, who was in charge of Reading (sc. Boys) School for more than 50 years, who flourished in the highest praise of the mind, of learning, of benevolence, who achieved a unique reputation of fame through his writings and his teaching experience, who formed his pupils, who came here most frequently, towards humanity, virtue, piety, most faithfully, through his care and his instructions, himself both an example and teacher of all skills and virtues. Several of his pupils took care of the execution of this, as a monument of their teacher (nay, blessed guardian), in grateful memory.'

'He died in Christ in London on the 28th of March, AD 1836, aged 81, and is buried in the suburban cemetery at Harrow Road.'

Inscription above the doorframe:

Valet Pietas.
'Piety is strong.'

Born in Jersey in 1754, Richard Valpy was appointed headmaster of Reading School in 1781. Under his leadership the school achieved an exceptionally good reputation, but Valpy is also remembered for his being 'one of the hardest floggers of his day' (Dictionary of National Biography).

Valpy was an enthusiast of Greek, Latin, and English literature (poetry and drama in particular), and his writings, including grammar books, achieved widespread acclaim.

Valet pietas is the family motto of the Valpy family. Note how the first syllables of each word, when combined, make up the sound of the name VAL-PY.

26. Foundation Stone of Kendrick School

A sizeable, grey–beige commemorative plaque, with an inconspicuous carved frame, can be seen on the outside wall of the Great Hall of Kendrick School. On the other side of the same wall, inside the Great Hall, there is an oil painting of John Kendrick, retrieved from Reading's workhouse – 'The Oracle'. He was the famous London cloth merchant who bequeathed the means by which Kendrick School was eventually founded (and who is mentioned in the inscription, alongside his wife Mary).

Posuit hunc lapidem angularem
Scholae in usum Redingensium Puellarum
e testamentis Joannis et Mariae Kendrick
olim fundatae et jam iterum aedificatae
Josephus Wells
Universitatis Oxoniensis vice-cancellarius
ipse Redingensis
a(nte) d(iem) XIII Kal(endas) Mart(is) a(nni) s(ancti) MCMXXVI.

'This cornerstone of the school, once founded towards the use of the Girls of Reading from the estate of John and Mary Kendrick and now re-built, was laid by Joseph Wells, vice-chancellor of the University of Oxford, himself a Readingite, on 17th of February, 1926.'

The Oracle workhouse was funded from John Kendrick's estate after his death in 1624. Following the closure of the workhouse, the remaining funds from his bequest were used to found Kendrick Girls School in 1877. (Kendrick Boys School was founded simultaneously; this school later became part of Reading School.) John Kendrick was the brother of William Kendrick, whose funerary monument is on display in the Reading Minster (see inscription 40).

The original site of Kendrick Girls School was on Watlington Street. Some fifty years later, the school moved to its present site, situated on land between East Street, London Street, and Sidmouth Street.

The inscription commemorates this second phase of Kendrick School. Joseph Wells, a Classical scholar and then vice-chancellor of the University of Oxford (as well as a pupil of Reading School), was present for the ceremonial laying of the foundation stone. Kendrick Girls School opened at its present site in 1927.

1926 was an auspicious year for Reading as a place of education; only a few weeks after the foundation stone of Kendrick Girls School was laid on 17 March, the University of Reading received its Royal Charter.

27. The Blagrave Monument

This is a lavishly decorated and coloured funerary monument, affixed to the south wall of the main nave of St Laurence's church. Centrally, the monument displays a bust of John Blagrave (1560ish–1611), holding a globe and a quadrant. He is surrounded by named female allegorical figurines that hold three-dimensional shapes with their names inscribed: standing next to Blagrave's bust are *Tetrahedron* and *Cubus*, above that *Octahedron* and *Dodicadron*, crowned by *Isocaedron*.

Iohannes Blagravus
totus mathematicus cum
matre sepultus.

'A mathematician through and through, John Blagrave is buried (here) with his mother.'

A poem in (somewhat clunky) English verse follows the Latin inscription:

Here lyes his corpes, which living had a spirit,
Wherein all worthy knowledge did inherit,
By which with zeale our God he did adore,
Left for maidservants and to feed the poore.
His vertuous mother came of worthie race,
A Hungerford, and buried neere this place.
When God sent death their lives away to call,

OCTAHEDRON

ODZEDRON

DODICADRON

TETRARI DRON

CUBVS

IOHANNES BLAGRAVS
TOTVS MATHEMATICVM
MATRE SEPVLTVS

They lived beloved, and dyed bewayld of all.

Deseassed the IXth of August
Anno Domini MDCXI.

The son of John Blagrave of Bulmershe Court, Earley, and Anne Hungerford, John Blagrave was one of the most celebrated mathematicians of Elizabethan times, dubbed 'the flower of mathematicians of his age' by Anthony Wood. Residing at Southcote Manor, an estate off Reading's Bath Road, Blagrave was particularly well known for his work as a diallist and designer of complex, sophisticated astronomical instruments.

Blagrave's dwelling at Southcote Manor was later reported to be haunted by the spectre of John Blagrave, warning the manor's subsequent residents not to lay their hands on what he said was the rightful property of his nephew Daniel Blagrave, signatory of the death warrant of King Charles I, and to whom John had left the estate. The manor has long been demolished and the site is now occupied by a more recent building, but the moat survives to this day (see also inscription 50).

His importance as a mathematician aside, Blagrave was also a major local benefactor – an aspect that the inscribed poem touches upon. Blagrave left, in his will, a number of legacies for the benefit of the townspeople. Monies from his estate were also used to build 'Blagrave Piazza', a six-arch arcade that once adjoined the south wall of St Laurence's church. This is the same wall that, on the inside, exhibits the Blagrave monument.

28. Funerary Inscription for the Merrick Family

A lecture given by one Mr W. Wing on 12 November 1894, entitled 'Old Caversham', notes that '[i]n Caversham Church rest the remains of a scholar and poet who in his day had considerable fame. The Rev. James Merrick, b. 1720, d. 1769, resided here, and was responsible for the Latin inscription on the tablet to his parents' memory at the west end of the north aisle in the Church.'

This tablet still exists, framed and mounted to the wall, in the very same spot.

In memoriam
Joannis Merrick, M(edicinae) D(octor)
De Reading
Cuius eximias ingeni dotes
Multa industria multaque eruditione excultas
Commendavit humanitas singularis
Et amabilis quaedam morum simplicitas.
Vita laboriosissima utilissima
Pie et placide defunctus est
Die 5 Aprilis 1757 Aet(atis) 87.
Uxorem duxit Elizabetham
Filiam Richardi Lybbe
De Hardwick in Agro Oxon(iensi) Arm(ige)ri
Et Sophiae foeminae lectissimae
Thomae Tipping Equitis Aur(ati) filiae,
Insigni prudentia mulierem,
Moribus sanctissimis:
Ex qua octo suscepit liberos.
Franciscus, filius natu tertius, ob(ii)t 24 Maii, 1738, Aet(atis) 28.
Guilielmus, natu quartus, Coll(egii) Di(vi) Jo(hannis) Bapt(istae) Oxon(iensis) Soc(ius)
Ob(ii)t 8 Jan(uarii) 1741, Aet(atis) 24.
Anna, filia natu secunda, ob(ii)t 5 Nov(embri) 1760, Aet(atis) 47.
Qui omnes cum Anna Joannis Merrick M(edicinae) B(accalaurei)
Uxore charissima
(Quae obiit 3 Oct(obri) 1760, Aet(atis) 48)
Et infante Francisci filio,
Intus ad hunc parietem jacent.
Hic etiam, prope dilectos cineres, conditus est
Joannes Merrick, M(edicinae) B(accalaureus),
Filius Joannis et Elizabethae natu primus,
Defunctus 10 Nov(embri) 1764, Aet(atis) 60,

In memoriam
IOANNIS MERRICK M.D.
De READING,
Cujus eximios ingenii dotes
Multa eruditio, priscaque eruditione exculta,
Communicandi Benignitas singularis,
Et amabilis, quæ dicti morum simplicitas,
Vita laboriosissima, utilissima,
Pie et placide defunctus est,
Die 3 Aprilis, 1757. Et 87.
Uxorem duxit ELIZABETHAM,
filiam RICHARDI LYBBE
De HARDWICK in Agro OXON. Arm.
Et SOPHIÆ fœminæ lectissimæ,
THOMÆ TIPPING, Equitis Aur. filiæ,
Insigni prudentia mulierem,
Moribus sanctissimis.
Ex quâ octo suscepit liberos.
FRANCISCUS, filius natu tertius, ob. 24 Maii, 1758. Et 28.
GULIELMUS, natu quartus Coll. D. JO. BAPT. OXON. Soc.
Ob. 8 Jan. 1711. Et 24.
ANNA, filia natu secunda, ob. 5 Nov. 1760. Et 47.
Qui omnes, cum ANNÂ JOANNIS MERRICK, M.B.
Uxore charissimâ,
(Quæ obiit 3 Oct. 1760. Et 48)
Et infante FRANCISCI filio,
Intus ad hunc parietem jacent.
Hic etiam, prope dilectos cineres, conditus est
JOANNES MERRICK M.B.
Filius JOANNIS et ELIZABETHÆ natu primus,
Defunctus 10 Nov. 1764. Et 60.
Qui hoc animi erga parentes optime meritos
Cæterosque suos memoris monumentum
Extare voluit,
Matri suæ, quæ annos 84 prope compleverat,
Exiguo intervallo,
Quippe eodem anno, die tertio Aprilis, defunctæ
Superstes.

Qui hoc animi erga parentes optime meritos
Caeterosque suos memoris monumentum
Extare voluit,
Matri suae, quae annos 84 prope compleverat,
Exiguo intervallo,
Quippe eodem anno, die tertio Aprilis, defunctae,
Superstes.

'In memory of John Merrick, M.D., of Reading, whose outstanding gifts of his mind, adorned with much energy and much learnedness, were commended by a singular humaneness and a special, amiable simplicity. A most laborious, purpose-filled life he surrendered, piously and placidly, on the 5th day of April, 1757, aged 87. He had married Elizabeth – the daughter of Richard Lybbe, Esq., of Hardwick in Oxfordshire, and of Sophia, a most distinguished woman, the daughter of Thomas Tipping, Knight of the Golden Spur – a woman of outstanding prudence and a most saintly character, from whom he took eight children.

'Franciscus, the third-born son, died on 24th of May, 1738, aged 28;

'William, fourth-born, Fellow of St John's College, Oxford, died 8th of January, 1741, aged 24;

'Anna, second-born daughter, died 5th of November, 1760, aged 47.

'They all, together with Anna, the most beloved wife of John Merrick, M. B., (who died on 3rd of October, 1860, aged 48), and their infant boy Francis, lie interred here at this wall.

'Here, too, near those beloved ashes, is buried John Merrick, M. B., the first-born son of John and Elizabeth, who died 10th of November, 1764, aged 60, who wanted this monument of a spirit remembering the well deserving parents as well as his other relatives, to exist, surviving his mother, who had nearly completed 84 years, by but a short period of time, as she died, the very same year, on the third day of April.'

James Merrick, composer of the above epitaph, was not only a successful poet of his time, but also an important figure in the development of Classical scholarship, who produced translations of the psalms, indices to Ancient Greek authors, and annotations to books of the Christian bible.

29. Commemorative Plaque of Wantage Hall

A sizeable metal plaque can be seen in the quadrangle of Wantage Hall, mounted on the north wall and affixed to a stone support that stands out from surrounding red brickwork.

Aulam hanc
coniugis sui dignissimi
Collegii Universitatis apud Radingam olim praesidis
nomini semper servando
d(onum) d(edit)
Baronissa de Wantage
MCMVIII
in usum iuventutis
studiis ibi liberalibus operaturae
ut communi ardore alacri sermone
in beatam litterarum ac scientiae sodalitatem
feliciter congregentur.

'This hall, to preserve the name of her most worthy husband, former president of University College, Reading, was given as gift by Baroness Wantage in 1908, for the use of the young, to engage in liberal study there, so they, in common ardour and eager speech, may fruitfully assemble for the blessed community of letters and science.'

In order to facilitate students moving away from home to study, Reading, like most other universities, began to offer halls of residence. The oldest hall of residence at Reading is Wantage Hall, on Upper Redlands Road, halfway between the University's original London Road campus and the Whiteknights estate, which is now the main campus of the University.

The building of Wantage Hall became possible due to the generosity of Baroness Wantage, widow of Robert Lloyd-Lindsay, 1st Baron Wantage, who had been president of University College, Reading. The foundation of Wantage Hall by Baroness Wantage, in memory of her husband, was commemorated for future generations in an inscription on a large bronze tablet, for all visitors to see, in the main quadrangle of the Hall.

Approximately one hundred years have passed since Wantage Hall first opened its doors to Reading students and this inscription was designed to commemorate this significant step in Reading's local history. The aspirations expressed in this inscription are no less relevant or important now than they were in 1908. The Higher Education sector in Britain has recently been obsessed with notions such as employability and transferable skills, and with the funding of the university system. It might be a good idea to remind ourselves of what the far wider mission of a university is supposed to be – and this commemorative plaque captures that idea in its very essence.

30. Latin Motto of St Patrick's Hall

This inscribed circular relief is inserted into the brick wall of the southeastern house front of Pearson Court, St Patrick's Hall, University of Reading, on Northcourt Avenue. The stone relief, representing a circle with four beams extending from it to form a cross, depicts two snakes, arranged in a circle, biting each other's tails – a symbol of eternity called *ouroboros* or 'tail eater' – and encircling a flame that emerges from a vessel.

> *Facta, non forma.*
>
> 'Deeds, not image.'

The imagery of this relief invokes the legend of St Patrick, patron saint of St Patrick's Hall – the same St Patrick who is reported to have driven the snakes out of Ireland.

As for the fire symbolism, according to pagan Irish belief, it was unlawful to light a fire on the hill of Tara on the eve of the Druid spring festival, at which time a special fire was lit there. On one occasion, however, St Patrick and his followers arrived first and lit a Paschal fire there. The Druid arch-priest told the king, and consequently the king ordered that the offenders should be instantly brought before him for

punishment. Upon interrogation, St Patrick then proclaimed to them that he had come to quench the fires of pagan sacrifice and light the flame of Christian faith in Ireland.

The inscription, much like its counterpart in Wantage Hall (29), is a reminder to its student readers to focus on deeper truths and meaningful action instead of pursuing mere appearances.

31. Funerary Plaque for John Taylor, MD

This marble plaque, in Reading Minster, is mounted on the wall to the right-hand side of the main entrance.

M(emoriae) S(acrum).
Joannis Taylor, M(edicinae) D(octoris)
Qui in hoc oppido plusquam L annos vixit
ob summam medicae artis peritiam
nemini non notus,
ob singularem animi candorem,

M.S.

JOANNIS TAYLOR, M.D.

QUI IN HOC OPPIDO PLUSQUAM L. ANNOS VIXIT,
OB SUMMAM MEDICÆ ARTIS PERITIAM
NEMINI NON NOTUS,
OB SINGULAREM ANIMI CANDOREM,
URBANAM MORUM SIMPLICITATEM, FACILEM COLLOQUII SUAVITATEM,
NEMINI NON DILECTUS.
FAMAM MERERI QUAM APPETERE MALUIT,
LENI ERGO LAPSU AD EXTREMAM SENECTUTEM DEVENIT
MENTEM, DOCTRINÂ ET LITERIS,
GRÆCIS PRÆCIPUE ET LATINIS, EXIMIE ADORNATAM,
AC SACRORUM LIBRORUM STUDIO DILIGENTER EXCULTAM,
SANAM AC INTEGRAM USQUE AD LXXXIV.ᵐ ANNUM SERVAVIT,
ET E PLACIDÂ TANDEM VITÂ PLACIDE DECESSIT
SPE FRETUS MELIORIS ET DIUTURNÆ.
NAT: A.D. MDCCXLI.   OB: A.D. MDCCCXXV.

urbanam morum simplicitatem, facilem colloquii suavitatem
nemini non dilectus,
famam mereri quam appetere maluit.
Leni ergo lapsu ad extremam senectutem devenit
mentem, doctrina et litteris
Graecis praecipue et Latinis eximie adornatam,
ac sacrorum librorum studio diligenter excultam,
sanam ac integram usque ad LXXXIVm annum servavit
et e placida tandem vita placide decessit
spe fretus melioris et diuturnae.
Nat(us) A(nno) D(omini) MDCCXLI. Ob(iit) A(nno) D(omini) MDCCCXXV.

'Sacred to memory. John Taylor, M.D., who lived in this town for more
than fifty years – well-known to everyone for his exceptional capacity in
medical science, well-beloved by everyone for the unique candour of his
mind, his humble, urban character, and the easy sweetness of his con-
versation: he preferred to earn recognition rather than to strive for it.
Thus, in a gentle slope he reached the highest age. Adorned with learnedness and literature: Greek, most of all, and Latin to the highest extent,
and also diligently cultivated by means of studying the sacred book, he
preserved a sane and intact mind to his 84th year. A placid life he aban-
doned placidly eventually, in deep trust for an even better and eternal
one. Born A.D. 1741. Died A.D. 1825.'

John Taylor was born in Manchester and educated at Brasenose College, Oxford. He lost his only son, Lieut.-Col. Taylor, in 1808 at the battle of Vimeiro, fighting for Gen. Arthur Wellesley in the Peninsular War.

The *Gentlemen's Magazine* of 1825 reports that Taylor was 'distinguished for skill, attention, and success. To the poor his advice and assistance were gratuitously rendered, and his private charities were extensive.' At Brasenose College, he 'acquired a high character for learning and general knowledge, and proceeded A. M. 1766; M. B. 1769, and M. D. 1780.'

32. The Motto of John Cecil Grainger

This armorial achievement, made of metal, is fixed to an obelisk in Reading Old Cemetery, Cemetery Junction. The arms are mounted on the pedestal of the obelisk that is a monument for John Cecil Grainger, once vicar of St Giles-in-Reading, and his wife.

The armorial achievement consists of a shield, a helmet, a crest (a stag with an ear of wheat – the abundance of wheat here and in the shield may well be a reference to the family name, Grainger), and the motto scroll.

The shield is rather complex. It is divided into a *dexter* (the left half of the shield for the viewer) and a *sinister* (the right), the latter of which is subdivided further. The dexter exhibits three ears of wheat, stalked and leaved, two over one. The sinister consists of four quarters. The first and fourth quarters display the same content – a chevron between three *pheons* (a type of arrow often used as a heraldic device). These may be a reference to the Smart of Trewhitt family, mentioned in the wife's inscription at the back of the monument. Two human shinbones in saltire feature in the second quarter, and a demi-lion rampant in the third quarter.

Both funerary inscriptions on this monument are written in English; the motto scroll of the arms is in Latin.

Defessus sum ambulando.

'I am worn out from all this walking about.'

Considering the genre – a motto scroll – the text conveys an unusual, in fact rather remarkable, level of resignation (not least for a parish priest). Why such a seemingly dispiriting motto?

The answer is somewhat surprising: to the knowing, the motto is not actually dispiriting at all. It is a verbatim reference to the play *Adelphoe* ('The Brothers') by the Roman second-century-BC playwright Terence. Demea, an older man and country-dweller, had been sent on a wild goose chase throughout the entire town by the slave Syrus, trying to find his brother Micio. When Demea finally gives up his attempt to find Micio according to the slave's instructions, he returns to the scene and says:

'I am worn out from all this walking about. Syrus, may the big Jupiter himself destroy you and your directions! I crawled through the entire town: to the gate, to the lake – where didn't I go? He did not have any workshop there, nor did anyone suggest to have seen my brother. Now I'll wait at home, I've decided, until he comes back.' (*Adelphoe* 713-8)

In keeping with the comic genre, as soon Demea gives up, of course, he finally gets to see Micio, who had been in the house all along (and who enters the stage just after Demea has finished his last line).

'Seek, and ye shall find,' they say – but a possible lesson from the scene above is that you cannot trust the directions given to you; go to the most likely place and pause, and what you are looking for will come to you. This may be the true idea behind the motto of John Cecil Grainger's arms, then – not resignation, but the deeper lesson that the suspension of restless activity and unplanned business may in fact be the better way to achieve one's aims.

A Dead Language for the Dead

Every culture and society has its own ways of honouring its ancestors and commemorating the dead. This may range from an unsentimental disposal of the body (as a health hazard) to commemoration through ritualised ceremonies and lavish monuments.

Focus may change of course from the funeral ceremony to competition for the most impressive monument – and this variation seems to cut across time, space, and social class. The desire to achieve a lasting memory, for oneself or ones relatives, combined with the use of inscribed funerary monuments, has, however, been a constant feature of European culture since ancient times.

This section covers inscriptions that testify to the universality of the desire not to be forgotten. This is true for the second- or third-century tombstone from Roman North Africa (inscription 33, now in Reading's Ure Museum of Greek Archaeology), just as much as for the monuments that are found in Reading's old parish churches of St Laurence, St Giles-in-Reading, and the Reading Minster, or the funerary texts that were mentioned in earlier sections, such as inscriptions 10, 11, and 17.

Many of the inscriptions are much more than just burial markers. They are expressions of hopes and desires for the afterlife, just as much as exhortations to those who were left behind or generations to come. They are manifestations of the wish of those from the past to speak to the world of the living, communicating virtues, ideals, and aspirations – and demanding a certain respect for their achievements.

Many of the Latin inscriptions collected here are much wordier than their English counterparts – for unknown reasons. Did the writers feel that they could encode their family history into Latin more comfortably, knowing that fewer people would be able to read it? A particularly interesting example of this is inscription 46, for which an English inscription exists as well. Or did the use of Latin make this form of self-representation more acceptable?

What is perhaps unsurprising, yet striking, is that, apart from the Roman tombstone, those who do get commemorated in Latin seem to be members of an educated elite, locally or more generally. They are noblemen and -women, politicians, clergymen, doctors. This does not mean, however, that all members of those groups in Reading chose to represent themselves in Latin – quite the contrary.

What they and their relatives chose to commemorate in the inscriptions often includes ideals and behaviours, in particular their self-professed roles as public benefactors and generous supporters of the poor – work done for the benefit of those who are least likely to be able to read about it in Latin. This raises an important question: if these monuments are not (just) about boasting in a public setting, with whom do they wish to communicate? Could it be that this was intended to encourage further competition among those who could read Latin as well as afford to follow suit?

If that is the case, handing down these texts to posterity – and crossing the language barrier – seems all the more important for present times.

33. A Roman Tombstone from Leptis Magna

This grey limestone slab, discovered in Leptis Magna, Libya, dates to the second or third century AD. It has countersunk panels with a double frame on all four sides, inscribed on the front, and is on display in the Ure Museum of Greek Archaeology in the Department of Classics at the University of Reading (Whiteknights Campus, Humanities and Social Sciences Building).

Domitiae Rogatae.
Vixit
annis XXIII.
M(arcus) Iulius
Cethegus
Phelyssam uxori
carissimae fecit.

'To Domitia Rogata.
She lived
twenty-three years.
Marcus Iulius Cethegus
Phelyssam had this made
for his most beloved wife.'

Both the honorand and the dedicator have names that are an indication of their northern African origin. Domitia Rogata's second name, *Rogata*, translates as 'Asked-For', indicating her parents' desire for a child, asking for divine support and expressing their doing so in their child's name, in keeping with a regional tradition. Her husband's name is typically Roman at first: *Marcus Iulius Cethegus* are the three names (*tria nomina*) of a free male Roman citizen. The fourth component, *Phelyssam*, however, seems to be a Berber name, reminiscent of a local Romanised Libyan population.

Perhaps the most noteworthy aspect of this inscription is its formal design. The letter size changes and decreases from top to bottom. The first three lines of letters resemble brushstrokes, so-called *actuaria* script. The next two lines appear in the well-known, monumental *capitalis quadrata* script. In the final two lines, the text reverts to the *actuaria* type.

The stonecutter laid out the text so that it both gradually draws the reader closer into the text (the final two lines cannot be easily read from afar) and reflects the inscription's contents in its formal design. In particular, the two lines that contain the dedicator's Roman *tria nomina* – the Roman part of his name-related identity – appear in the typical script of Roman monuments. The two lines that contain Cethegus' regional identity, as well as the most personal part of his message remembering his late wife, are written in small, casual letters, visible only to a reader who makes an effort to come closer and probably kneel down at the stone.

34. Funerary Plaque for John and Joan Kent

This engraved and partly restored brass inlay of a gravestone, removed from its original setting in the late nineteenth century and preserved in a wooden frame, is now attached to the north wall of the north aisle of St Laurence's church.

Hic iacent Joh(ann)es Kent quondam Burgensis de Redyng et
Johanna uxor eius, quor(um) a(n)i(m)abus p(ro)picietur deus. Amen.

'Here lie John Kent, once a Burgess of Reading, and his wife, Joan. May God have mercy on their souls. Amen.'

John Kent was a Reading-based mercer and politician in the late four-teenth to early fifteenth century. In particular, he served as tax collector, five times mayor, bailiff, and coroner.

Kent also was a major benefactor of St Laurence's church, where he was buried under a marble gravestone in the chancel after his death in 1413.

A possible son and grandson of the Kents went into politics as well. A Simon Porter, alias Kent, was mayor of Reading, and John Kent, who was mayor of Winchester, was reportedly the son of a Simon Kent of Reading.

35. Brass Plaque for William Baron

A late medieval bronze tablet, originally mounted on a gravestone, is now inserted in a wooden frame and mounted on the outside of the east wall of the south aisle of Reading Minster, to the right of the entrance to the Lady chapel. The text is engraved in a Gothic script.

Hic iacit Will(ia)m(u)s Baron(us) qui obiit quarti die mensis Martii
Anno d(omi)ni MCCCCXVI, cuius anime p(ro)picietur deus. Amen

'Here lies William Baron, who died on the fourth day of March, AD 1416. May god have mercy on his soul. Amen.'

There was a William Baron, Esquire, of Reading, who was one of the Tellers of the Exchequer. He was born around 1410, and in the early 1430s he married Joan Knollys, daughter of Thomas Knollys, Sheriff and Lord Mayor of London. The 'History of the Family of Wrottesley' reports him to be 'the head of an ancient family which had been settled for many years in Berkshire'.

It would seem to be beyond reasonable doubt that the William Baron in the Latin inscription of Reading Minster belongs to an earlier generation of the same family.

36. Funerary Poem for John Andrew

This late medieval bronze tablet is mounted on a gravestone in the chancel of St Laurence's church, just outside the rails of the high altar. The gravestone once also exhibited a brass shield and the effigy of a priestly figure, both of which are now missing. The text is engraved in a Gothic script, and the lines of the inscription are arranged in pairs, emphasised by brackets engraved to the right of the text as well as by the varying rhythmical patterns (an initial elegiac distich is followed by two hexameters and two lines in prose). The four initial, poetic lines of the text are 'Leonine verse', that is, they show internal and line-final rhyming patterns.

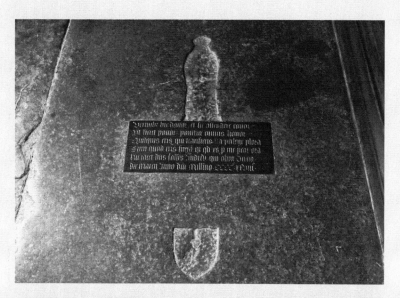

Vermib(u)s hic donor: et sic ostendere conor
ut sicut ponor, ponitur omnis honor.
Quisquis eris qui transieris sta, perlege, plora.
Sum quod eris fuera(m)q(u)e quod es. p(ro) me, pr(ec)or, ora.
Hic iacet d(omin)us Joh(ann)es Andrew qui obiit tercio
die Marcii Anno d(o)m(ini) Mill(esi)mo CCCCo XXVIIIo.

'This is a gift to the worms: thus, too, I try to show that, just as I am deposited, all honour is deposited. Whoever you will be, passing by: stand still, read, and weep: I am what you will be, and I was what you are. Please, pray for me. Here lies John Andrew, who died on the third day of March, AD 1428.'

The only truly individual part of this inscription is the two final, non-poetic lines: the first couplet occurs many times in medieval and early modern Latin inscriptions from both Britain and the continent. It also famously features in *La danse macabre des femmes* ('The Women's Dance of Death'), a fifteenth-century French poem that would be roughly contemporary with the inscription.

The second pair of lines, asking the passer-by to engage with the inscription and its monument and pointing out the fleeting nature of life, resembles a notion common in ancient Latin inscriptions.

Considering that John Andrew was a man of the cloth (as the priestly effigy that was once mounted to his gravestone suggests), the somewhat disenchanted fatalism displayed in this inscription seems rather extraordinary. Just over sixty years before he died, however, Reading had lived through the plague, a disease that killed the Abbot of Reading at that time, Henry of Appleford (d.1361). Death, decay, and rotting bodies would therefore have still been very much a part of living memory.

37. Funerary Inscription for John Popham, Kt.

This late medieval bronze tablet is inscribed in a Gothic script. Originally mounted on a gravestone, the tablet has been inserted in a metal frame on hinges and mounted on the wall at the west end of the main nave of St Laurence's church, next to the entrance to the church tower.

Hic iacet Joh(ann)es Popham miles qu(on)d(a)m d(omi)n(u)s de Turney in Normandia et d(omi)n(u)s
de Chardeford, de Dene, ac de Abyngton et alibi in Anglia, qui obiit XIIIIo die mens(is) Aprilis Anno d(omi)ni Mill(esi)mo CCCCo LXIIIo, cui(us) a(n)i(m) e p(ro)piciet(ur) de(us).

'Here lies John Popham, Knight, once Lord of Tournai-Sur-Dive in Normandy and Baron of Char(de)ford, Dean, and Abington and elsewhere in Anglia, who died on the 14th day of the month of April, AD 1463. May god have mercy on his soul.'

Sir John Popham (c. 1395–1463) was a high-ranking military commander and diplomat of the fifteenth century, and the presence of his funerary inscription in Reading is the result of a truly remarkable story.

The son of Sir John Popham and his wife Matilda (presumably the daughter of Oliver Zouche of South Charford), John Popham soon became a successful military man. He served on the 1415 campaign for Edward, Duke of York, whose manor of Vastern (Wootton Bassett) he inhabited after the duke's death. He was knighted around the time of the battle of Agincourt during the Hundred Years' War.

Popham's continued success did not escape the attention of King Henry V, and resulted in generous honours and prestigious appointments. Following Henry's death in 1422, Popham became chancellor of France (or of Normandy), and continued to fight in the Hundred Years' War (e.g. in the defence of Paris, following the successes of Jeanne d'Arc, in 1429).

In England, Popham eventually became Treasurer of the Household and MP for Hampshire. He was even nominated to become the Speaker in 1449, but declined due to ill health. In 1460, Popham was admitted to the confraternity of London Charterhouse. After his death in 1463, he was buried in the Charterhouse chapel that he endowed.

So how did the inscription of this remarkable man end up in Reading? The answer to this question must lie in the burial spot that was chosen for him; the monastery of London Charterhouse was closed under Henry VIII in 1537 and sold in 1545, after which the building was transformed.

In the context of this shake-up, the metal plaque that once marked the grave of Sir John Popham must have been sold to an engraver, and it was subsequently re-used for the inscription of Walter Barton (d. 1538) on the other side of the plaque – see inscription 38.

John Popham's inscription was rediscovered when Rev. Charles Kerry (who wrote an 1883 history of St Laurence's church) suspected Barton's inscription to be a 'rescript' and had it removed from its marble slab near the altar of St Laurence's. It was later mounted on the wall as described above, for both sides of the brass to remain visible. The same solution was found for the effigies that came with the inscription.

38. Funerary Inscription for Walter Barton

This late medieval bronze tablet, inscribed in a Gothic script, was originally mounted on a gravestone near the altar. It is now inserted in a metal frame on hinges, mounted on the wall at the west end of the main nave of St Laurence's church, next to the entrance to the church tower. (For a fuller account of this brass's history, see inscription 37.)

Here und(e)r this m(a)rble stone lieth Water Barton, gent., Which dece-sid ye
XXV day of Apryll in the yere of our lord God M'DXXXVIII on
Whos soule And all Crysten Soules Th(o)u have mercy AMEN.
Celeste(m) quo(n)da(m) vita(m) qui duxerat, ista : verm(i)b(u)s ecce sta(n)tes
: ia(m) req(u)`i´escit humo.

Wa(l)ter Barton, who in the English part of this inscription is referred to as a 'gentleman', appears to have been a tradesman, and he is listed as churchwarden of St Laurence's in 1509.

The inscription blends English and Latin. The English part in the first three lines contains all essential information and wishes for Barton, fol-lowed by a single Latin line that expresses a more general sentiment in a short poem. The Latin is faulty and almost nonsensical, resulting in an equally faulty rhythmical two-line pattern known as the *elegiac distich* (with its subdivision highlighted by means of punctuation in the inscription):

Celeste(m) quo(n)da(m) vita(m) qui duxerat, ista:
verm(i)b(u)s ecce sta(n)tes: ia(m) req(u)`i´escit humo.

'He who once had led a heavenly life, this
to the worms, behold, standing: already he rests in the earth.'

This ought to have been an expression of the idea that Barton's mor-tal remains are now feeding the worms (*vermibus ecce cibus*), similar to that in the inscription for John Andrew (36), situated in the vicinity of this one.

39. Funerary Monument for Thomas Lydall

This complex funerary monument, with traces of colour remaining, is attached to the north wall of the north aisle of St Laurence's church. Between three black Corinthian columns, which form two arched niches, there are two sculpted scenes: to the left, there is a kneeling man, with three boys behind him; to the right, there is a kneeling woman, with six girls behind her. Both the man and the woman, thus represented as father and mother, kneel at a desk of the of the prie-dieu type, facing each other. The monument dates to the early 1600s, and it was originally inserted over the chancel door (from where it was moved a number of times before arriving in its present location).

Both scenes have very faded Latin inscriptions placed below them. The text is a two-part poem, one for each of the two parental figures.

a. Left-hand side

Quam fuerat vita charus, quam morte Lydallus,
narret pastor, plebs, pauper, et ista domus.
ista domus testis pietatis, pauper amoris,
plebs operum, fidei pastor, in hisque deus.

'How dear Lydall was in life, how dear in death, explain the priest, the people, the pauper, and this house. This house testifies to his piety, the pauper to the love, the people to his achievements, to his faith the priest, and in these is God.'

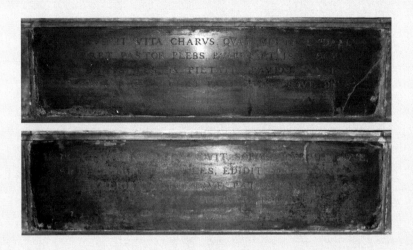

b. Right-hand side

Hanc, lector, bene qui novit, sobolemque virumque
saepe hos, aut similes, edidit ore sonos:
o ter felicem matremque patremque propago
cui tali ex tali conjuge talis erat.

'Who knew her well, Reader, as well as her offspring and her husband, many a time has uttered these (or similar) words: o thrice lucky mother and father, who as such, from such a partner, had such offspring.'

In its original context, the monument was accompanied by a further inscription, also written in Latin. This is now lost, and the line divisions remain unclear, as those sources that reproduce the text do not agree:

Est hoc, candide inspector, Thomae Lydall generosi majoratum apud Redingenses ter perfuncti (qui domus huius sacrae concionatoris pauperumque auxit reditus) et Margeriae uxoris et liberorum pie consecratum memoriae monumentum.

'This is, esteemed beholder, a monument piously consecrated to the memory of Thomas Lydall, generous three-times holder of the mayoralty with the people of Reading (who increased the revenues of the priest of this holy building as well as that of the poor) and Margery, his wife, and his children.'

Thomas Lydall, the male recipient of this monument, was a mercer by trade. He was born in 1550 and died in 1608. His wife, Margery Lydall (née Thorpe), whom he married in 1582, was born in 1555 and died in 1614.

As displayed in the relief, they had three sons (Thomas, Edward, and Richard) and six daughters, not all of whom appear to be commemorated by name. One of the daughters, Jane Lydall, married William Kendrick, the honorand of the Kendrick monument (see inscription 40), in 1606.

40. The Kendrick Monument

This complex funerary monument, mainly designed in black and gold, is attached to the north wall of the chancel of Reading Minster. The central part of the monument depicts two figures – William Kendrick and his wife – kneeling at a prie-dieu type desk, facing each other.

Above, a structure with an arch at the top and a golden garland at the bottom, crowned by three golden skulls, contains an escutcheon combining the family arms of the Kendrick and the Lydall family, as well as a motto scroll at its centre. The motto is *Dum spiro spero*, 'While I breathe, I hope.'

Below the central part sits a square black panel, inscribed with golden letters.

Guliel(mus) Kendricke,
Ex hinc resurget ad novissimae tubae sonitum
Vir faelix genere,
Avitis eiusdem nominis Regibus Saxonicis oriundus,
Faelix consanguineis,
Fratre praesertim Iohanne, Mercatore Londinensi, Cuius in hoc
oppidum merita, et in pauperes munificentiam, nec praesens aetas
imitata est, nec facile credet futura.
Felix maritus,
Matronam post se relinquens castissimam, pientissimam.
Faelix pater,
Natam sortitus caelis paratissima⟨m⟩, ad quos (!) praem⟨i⟩sit; qui et
in Filio unigenito, nepotibusq(ue) pluribus, se funeri sensit sup(er)stitem,
et ad saecula transmissum nascitura.
Faelix magistratu,
(Quem sibi aegre quidem ferenti demandatum) sum⟨m⟩a cum pruden-
tia, cura, authoritate, decor⟨e⟩, administravit.
U⟨nde⟩quaq(ue) demum Faelix,
Nisi quod vesicae dolores acutissimi autumnum vitae fecerant
Valetudinarium, et prorsus afflictissimum: sed et hinc
Cessit in exemplum mirae tolerantiae.
Naturae concessit, Marti 16o, anno salut(is) 1635, aetat(is) 56. Im<m>en-
sum sui apud bonos inopesq(ue), relinquens desideriu<m>.

'William Kendrick will rise from here to the sound of the last trumpet, a man blessed with pedigree, offspring of forefathers of the same name that were Saxon kings; blessed with his family, his brother in particular, John, merchant of London, whose merits towards this town, and whose munificence towards the poor, is unrivalled in the present time, and hard to believe for the future; blessed as a husband, leaving behind a wife most chaste, most pious; blessed as a father, who was allotted a daughter, most prepared for the Heavens, whither she was sent ahead, and who felt that he survives death through his sole son, and several grandchildren, handed down to posterity; blessed with public office (which he accepted, if grudgingly, and handled with highest prudence, care, authority, and to its adornment); finally, blessed in every regard, except that the most acute pains of the bladder [or: gall bladder] turned the autumn of his life to a sick-bed of utter suffering: but even from there he left as an example of remarkable tolerance. He gave in to nature on 16th of March, AD 1635, aged 56, leaving behind an immense desire for himself with the Good as well as with the Poor.'

William Kendrick, whose inscription asserts descendance from King Cynric of Wessex (who ruled 534–560), was born 15 October 1577, the son of Reading cloth merchant Thomas Kendrick and his wife Agnes.

He was the younger brother of Reading's patron John Kendrick (1573–1624), the sponsor of Reading's Oracle workhouse and, indirectly, of the Kendrick schools (see inscription 26). It is reported that William suggested the name for the workhouse.

In 1606, William Kendrick married Jane Lydall, daughter of Thomas Lydall (see inscription 39). Like his relatives, a clothier by trade, William Kendrick was a major benefactor of Reading and its parishes. He was mayor of Reading in 1632, and had served as churchwarden of Reading Minster from 1607 to 1610.

As reported in the inscription, William and Jane Kendrick had two children, a daughter called Elizabeth (who died young) and a son called Thomas.

William Kendrick was laid to rest under a marble stone whose inscription is reported as follows (note that the year is 1634, not 1635, as in the monument!):

Here under lyeth the Body of William Kendrick, gent., late maior of Reading, who was buried March 24, 1634.

The position of this stone is unclear; some report it as 'on the south side of Reading Minster', whereas others locate it 'within the rails of the altar'. This is the point of reference for the monument, when it expresses the belief that William Kendrick shall rise *ex hinc*, 'from here', to the sound of the last trumpet. This is a reference to 1 Corinthians 15:52: 'in a moment, in the twinkling of an eye, at the last trumpet. For the trumpet will sound, and the dead will be raised imperishable, and we shall be changed'.

The Latin shows a surprising number of small mistakes in spelling, which may be the result of careless restoration. Earlier reports of the text show a substantially more correct version. This does not prove much, however, as these reports may tacitly have corrected the faulty language of the inscription without indicating they had done so.

41. Funerary Monument for Martha Hamley

This once colourful and lavish stone monument, now rather worn and cracked, is inserted in the south wall of the main nave of St Laurence's church. The monument displays a female figure, wearing hat and ruff, kneeling at a bench of the prie-dieu type. Below the central sculpture, there is an inscription.

Martha, uxor Caroli Hamley Cornub(iensis), hic iacet
sepulta. Filia erat Thomae Seakes de Henley sup(er)
Thamesin in comitat(u) Oxoniae, quae obiit decimo sexto
die mensis Ianuarii an(no) D(omi)ni 1636. Hoc monumentum
struxit eius maritus Carolus ad conservandam eius
memoriam quae liberos nullos post se reliquit,
praesertim vero in testimonium summae suae dilectionis.

'Martha, the wife of Charles Hamley of Cornwall, lies buried here. She was the daughter of Thomas Seakes of Henley-upon-Thames in Oxfordshire, who died on the sixteenth day of the month of January, AD 1636. This monument was erected by her husband Charles to preserve the memory of her, who did not leave behind any children, but particularly as a testimonial to his extraordinary affection.'

It was written in or around 1636 – in this year Charles I was king of England, the University of Oxford was given a Great Charter, granting it the right to print 'all manner of books', and Europe was in the middle of the Thirty Years' War.

Martha's inscription, like many others, talks about other people and those who were left behind just as much as about the deceased. The inscription claims to have been set up to commemorate Martha, yet one does not actually learn much about her, apart from her name, the names of her father and her husband, the childlessness of their marriage, and the claim that she was loved by her husband.

Other documents confirm that Martha's father, Thomas Seakes, was an apothecary in Henley-on-Thames. Her husband, Charles Hamley (from Cornwall), in records of the Corporation, is referred to as 'Mr Saunders's man', which appears to be a reference to one John Saunders, an influential man in politics at the time.

The husband, or so the text purports, had the monument erected for two reasons: first, to commemorate his wife *quae liberos nullos post se reliquit*, 'who did not leave behind any children' – one feels almost compelled to infer '*because* she did not leave behind any children'; secondly, because he loved her very much.

The way in which the inscription presents this matter, when taken in conjunction with the sculpture of a pious lady, might suggest that the couple's childlessness was a major issue during their lifetime and for their relationship. However, the inscription does not say so, and further research shows that one must be extremely cautious with such conclusions. As becomes clear, the reason for their childlessness was that Martha most likely died too young, perhaps – again, a wild claim, rooted in the fact that children are mentioned at all – in childbirth.

How do we know this? Archival research reveals that Martha Seakes married Charles Hamley in mid 1634, only about a year and a half before she died. Their marriage allegation (of 30 July 1634) is kept in the Marriage Bonds and Allegations records in the London Metropolitan Archives. The text suggests that Martha was 22 years old at the time. Her spouse was 31. If this is correct, one can infer that when Martha died in January 1636, she was only 23 or 24.

In this case, we must take the inscription at face value: the monument has been designed to extend the memory of Martha Hamley, taking on what would have been her progeny's task – to testify to their mother's virtues and achievements.

42. Funerary Monument for Thomas Kenton

This sizeable marble monument is mounted on the east wall of the south transept of St Giles-in-Reading, close to the entrance. The inscription is barely visible on a black oval area in the middle. It is framed by two columns, and crowned by the comparatively colourful arms above the monument.

Bonae memoriae
Thomae Kenton panarii
Hujus antiqui Municipii Redingiae
Senatoris, nec non anno MDCLXV
Praetoris dignissimi. Qui cum bona
Fide eademque prudentia iis honoribus
Functus fuisset, tandem placida piaque
Morte solutus, mortales reliquias, dum
Christo iubente resurgent immortales,
In hac ecclesia, hic juxta, deposuit.
Fuit Christianae religionis verus professor,
Pietatis et virtutum omnium cultor et amator.
Vixit rerum suarum vir studiosissimus, alieni indifferens.
Duas duxit uxores, sed nullos reliquit liberos.
Obiit die quarto mensis Octobris, A(nno) D(omi)ni MDCLXXIII.
Anna, uxor moestissima, hoc, veri amoris,
Et obsequii, bene merenti posuit
Monumentum.

'To the good memory of Thomas Kenton, baker, senator of this ancient township of Reading, and also Mayor in the year of 1665. Who in good faith, and with the same prudence, executed these offices, has, finally redeemed by a placid and pious death, deposited his mortal relics in this church, near this place, until they rise again in immortality, ordered by Christ. He was a true promoter of Christian religion, a cultivator and lover of piety and of all virtues. He lived his life as a man who was most attentive to his own affairs, indifferent towards those of others. He married twice, but did not leave behind any children. He died on the fourth day of October, AD 1673. Anna, his most saddened wife, has had this monument to true love and compliance erected for him, who was well-deserving.'

Several websites and leaflets claim that the Thomas Kenton of St Giles parish was a clothier, not a baker as stated by the inscription. This seems implausible, and the origin of this notion is hard to establish. Kenton's will and testament is held by the Public Record Office, and while it establishes him as a 'Gentleman', it does not establish his prime occupation as that of a 'clothier'.

There are, however, a number of people named Thomas Kenton known from mid-seventeenth century Reading. The Diary of Reading Corporation, 1634, mentions one Thomas Kenton, 'servant to Mr John Castell', who was subject to legal proceedings:

'Margaret Abrey, spinster, complayneth that she is with childe begotten by Thomas Kenton, servant to Mr. John Castell, of Readinge, for he had carnall knowledge of her bodye in his lodgeinge chamber, in Mr. John Castell's house at Caversham, they beinge both servantes to Mr. Castle, in barley harvest last past and at other tymes since, promisinge her mariage. The said Thomas Kenton confesseth he had the use of her body about that tyme, but never promised her mariage.'

Some ten years earlier, another (or the same?) character named Thomas Kenton is mentioned in the Diary:

'At this day the freemen Coblers complayned that John Bartholmewe hath enterteyned and harbored one Thomas Kenton, a forreyner, a fortnighte against the orders of the towne, at iijd. a weeke. And that the said Thomas Kenton keepeth a shoppe and worketh as a Cobler freman, and hath soe done ever synce Christmas last: forbidden.'

The Diary of 1645 mentions, on a number of occasions, one 'Thomas Kenton, a younge clothier' as a suitor.

A Thomas Kenton, Yeoman of Reading, whose will dates to 1611, died too early to be the honorand of the St Giles monument, but he would seem to be of the same family of Reading dignitaries.

43. Gravestone for Edward Dalby

This gravestone is now in the graveyard of St Laurence's church, just north of the church building. The stone was originally placed near the altar of the church, but was moved outside when refurbishment took place.

Spe resurgendi
Hic prope depositi sunt cineres Edwardi Dalby,
ar(miger) qui obiit 30 Martii, Anno D(omi)ni 1672,
aetatis 56.
Et Franciscae uxoris ejus, filiae superstitis et her(e)dis
Caroli Holloway, ar(miger), servientis ad legem:
Haec obiit 17 Augusti, anno D(omi)ni 1717,
aetatis 90.
Et Elizabethae, filiae eorundem, quae obiit
8 Februarii, anno D(omi)ni 1686, aetatis 23.

'In the hope of resurrection, here are deposited the ashes of Edward Dalby, Esq., who died 30th of March, AD 1672, aged 56. Also of Frances, his wife, surviving daughter and heir of Charles Holloway, Esq., serjeant-at-law: she died on 17th of August, AD 1717, aged 90. Also of Elizabeth, their daughter, who died on 8th of February, AD 1686, aged 23.'

The stone, embellished with a significant coat of arms at its top, and now exposed to weather, dirt and vegetation, records the life of Edward Dalby of the Inner Temple and the lives of his family. Edward was one of Reading's foremost dignitaries at the time.

Henry Hyde, Earl of Clarendon, described him as a man 'of eminent loyalty and as wise a man as I have known of his rank'. He married Frances, daughter of Charles Holloway, also a lawyer. Dalby became Recorder (or High Steward) of Reading in 1669, replacing Daniel Blagrave, who had to flee the country for his involvement in regicide. Daniel had been one of the signatories of King Charles I's death warrant; see also inscription 27.

Spe   Resurgend

...li prope Depofiti Sunt Cineres... ...Richardi... ...rdi
Ar. Qui Obyt 30 Martis Anno D... ...

Ætatis...

Et Francifcæ Uxoris ejus... ...
Caroli Holloway Ar. ...
hæc Obyt 17 Augusti Anno Dni 1...

Ætatis 90...

Et Elizabethæ Filiæ corundem qui O...
...6 February Anno Dni 16.. ...tatis...

44. Gravestone for Francis and Elizabeth Hungerford

This sizeable gravestone, originally placed within the rails of the altar of St Laurence's church, was moved outside to the churchyard. The stone has subsequently been partly cut away, to make room for a small shack that has been added to the church wall.

Due to its continued mistreatment, as well as exposure to weather, the inscription is in a very poor state, with a large proportion of the text barely visible.

S(ubter) h(oc) s(axum)
Beatam anhelantes resuscitationem in vitam
aeternam, obdormiscunt
Franciscus Hungerford, M(edicinae) D(octor) et Elizabetha
uxor ejus, in agro Wilt(shire) utrique nati.
Ex qua suscepit ille septem filios,
et quinque filias, quorum decem supervixerunt
illi, parsque totius numeri dimidiata
quam proxime hic sepulta jacet.
Connubii inter eos vinculum, obstructum fuit
anno decollationis Caroli primi,
regis optimi et martyris:
dissolutum; primo, per uxoris interitum 1696:
annoque sequenti, mors, illum, meridie noctis
[integra, solute do]rmientem, in medela artem
[quasi pertimesc]ens, inopinanter arripuit.
[Edwardus filius e]orum unice superstes et heres
[pietatis et am]oris ergo hoc moerens posuit
1702.

[ille] (vacat) octogesimo || currente
[Obiit] (vacat) anno aetatis suae
illa (vacat) sexagesimo || sexto.

'Underneath this stone, desiring blessed resurrection to an eternal life, Francis Hungerford, MD and his wife Elizabeth have fallen asleep, both born in Wiltshire. He received seven sons from her, and five daughters, ten of which have survived him, and half of the total number lies buried here in close proximity. The bond of marriage between them was obstructed in the year of the decapitation of Charles I, the best king and martyr, and has then been dissolved: first, due to the death of the wife in 1696: then in the following year, death, almost afraid of his skills in curing, snatched him away, unsuspecting, in the middle of the night, while he slept soundly. Edward, their sole surviving son and heir, erected this out of filial dutifulness and love in sadness in 1702.

'He died during the eightieth year of his life, she died during the sixty-sixth year of her life.'

Francis Hungerford was a physician, and as the inscription points out playfully, clearly Death had to come at night, afraid of the daytime skills of this doctor. In fact, there are records that give an impression of the fame that Hungerford acquired – such as a treatise sent to him by one

Richard Griffiths, MD, entitled 'A-la-Mode Phlebotomy no good fashion; or the copy of a Letter to Dr. [Francis] Hungerford [of Reading], complaining of...the phantastick behaviour and unfair dealing of some London physitians... Whereupon a fit occasion is taken to discourse of the profuse way of Blood-Letting' (1681, mentioned in the Dictionary of National Biography).

The final years of the reign of King Charles I mark a troublesome time for Hungerford, who was clearly a loyal royalist, according to the wording of the inscription. Hungerford married his wife Elizabeth (née Keats) in December 1648, a time when Charles I had already been arrested by Parliament forces, and shortly before his execution on 30 January 1649.

This was not the only impact on Hungerford's life caused by the English Civil War. Hungerford was a Fellow of All Souls College, Oxford, and was expelled in 1647 'for non-submission to the authority of Parliament'.

The sole surviving son, Edward Hungerford, is commemorated as a major benefactor of the town and the parish on a surviving marble plaque that is mounted on the north wall of the north aisle of St Laurence's church.

45. Gravestone for John Hungerford

This grey marble gravestone is located in the south-eastern corner of the north chapel of St Laurence's church, and bears a substantial relief of the Hungerford coat of arms. The stone is now partly covered by the raised floor level resulting from the church's redevelopment in Victorian times, so the final line of its inscription is inaccessible.

Johannes Hungerford `Arm(ige)r´
de Blackland in Comitatu
Wilts(hire) hic jacet sepultus. Obijt
xxviijo Die Maij Anno
MDCLXXVIIJ.

'John Hungerford, Esq., of Blackland, in the county of Wiltshire, lies buried here. He died on the 28th of May, in the year 1678.'

John Hungerford, a barrister, was admitted to the Honourable Society of the Middle Temple, and called 'of Grace' in 1674. A marriage allegation issued by the Dean and Chapter of Westminster, for John to marry his wife, Mary, dates to 1677, only one year before his death. The relevant entry gives John Hungerford's age as 'about 28', meaning that he died aged 28 or 29. The couple had one daughter, also called Mary.

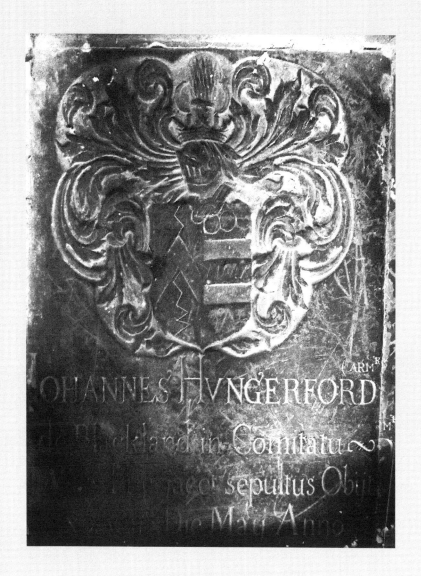

IOHANNES HVNGERFORD ARM[R]
...Buckland in Comitatu[M]
...Her...se[ci] sepultus Obijt
...Maij Anno

46. Funerary Monument of the Terrell Family

This sizeable marble monument is attached to the south wall of the main nave of St Giles-in-Reading.

In Memoriam
Optimorum Parentum Roberti & Ben(n)ett Terrell,
Quorum Ille
(Praefectus olim hujus Municipij integerrimus)
Familiam jacentem
Industria honestis Artibus, Paterno affectu
Diligentissime Fovit & Paululum erexit:
Haec, maturissima aetate, annorum nempe 89,
Deo devotissima, Liberis indulgentissima,
Pauperibus benignissima, Vicinis carissima
Defuncta est,
Ex Superstitibus Liberis Robertus & Franciscus
Hoc Monumentum
Gratitudinis pignus & amoris
Maerentes posuere
Anno Domini
1710.

Franciscus Filiorum alter
Post Annos Septuaginta Duos
Sine strepitu transitos
Animam Deo reddidit,
Martij 12o
1726.

'In memory of the best parents, Robert and Bennett Terrell, of whom he (a most upright mayor of this town some time ago) fostered with the greatest care a lowly family, with industriousness, honest work, and fatherly affection, and even helped them to rise a little bit: she died at a most mature age, in fact she was aged 89, a lady most devout to God, most indulgent to her children, most benign to the poor, most dear to her neighbours. Of their surviving children, Robert and Francis have set up this monument, in sadness, as a token of their gratitude and their love, in AD 1710.

'Francis, the second of the sons, returned his soul to God after seventy-two years spent without any fuss, on 12th of March, 1726.'

A second, English inscription in St Giles-in-Reading, not currently visible in the church, is reported for the parents:

'Here lyeth the body of Robert | Tirrell, who was mayor of Reading | in the year 1668, and departed this life the 25th | of July, Anno Domini 1679, | in the 59th year of his age. | And here also lyeth the body of | Bennett his wife, who departed | this life the 14th May, | Ann. D'ni 1710, | in the 89th year of her age.' (C. Coates, *The History and Antiquities of Reading*, 1802, p. 372)

The second inscription, on a gravestone, clearly corresponds with the monument mounted on the church wall (note, however, the inconsistency in the spelling of the family name). Interestingly, the Latin inscription is rather more generous in providing personal details of the family history of the parents, not least when it comes to detailing their lowly origins. Does that make the words of the Latin inscription 'privileged knowledge'?

Francis, the son who, curiously, is mentioned to have led a life 'without any fuss', was in fact mayor of Reading as well, just like his father, in 1680 and 1689.

47. Funerary Monument for Nathaniel Resbury

This marble plaque is set into a columned structure, with the family arms on top. It is mounted on the west wall of the north transept of St Giles-in-Reading.

H(ic) s(ubter) i(acet)
Nathaniel Resbury S(anctae) T(heologiae) P(rofessor).
Rector Ecclesiae D. Pauli ad Shadwel Lond(inii) Annis XXII
Wilhelmo tercio, Clarissimae Memoria<e> Regi
Nec non serenissmimae Reginae Annae, a Sacris.
Ob(iit) 21 Jul(ii) A(nno) D(omini) 1711o Aetat(is) LXVIII.

Eodem pariter in Sepulchro una conditur
(Morte non solvente vinculum)
Maria Vuxor eius non ita pridem praeiens
23 Mart(ii) A(nno) D(omini) 1710 Aetat(is) LXVIII.

Virum specta bonum, Theologum consummatum,
Concionatorem fervidum, pacificum mollientem,
Hinc inde contra Schismaticos ac pontificios
Suscepta Defensione Fidei,

Inter alios ad id munus evocatum
Pro parte sibi mandata Scriptorem strenuum,
Erga suos in sorte quidem tenui beneficum
In ampliori demum et erga alios magnificum,
In Dei quippe Gloriam et Emolumentum Ecclesiae
Legavit C libras Scholae ad Shadwel locatae
Pro pueris in Catechesi Eccl(esiae) Angl(icae) erudiendis.
Operatus bonum ad o(mn)es, maxime ad Domesticos Fidei,
Tempore suo metit, utpote qui non defecit.

Vade, Lector, et fac similiter.

'Here below lies Nathaniel Resbury, Doctor of Divinity, Rector of St Paul's Church, Shadwell, for 22 years, chaplain in ordinary to William III, a king of outstanding fame, as well as to the very fair Queen Anne. He died 21st of July, 1711, aged 68.

'Together with him, in the same vault (death did not loosen the bond they tied), lies Mary, his wife, who went ahead, if not by much, on 23rd of March, 1710, aged 68.

'Behold a good man, a consummate theologian, a fervid preacher, a soothing reconciler, equally against the schismatics and the papists in his defence of faith, called forward among others to this assignment; a strenuous writer for the task that was handed to him, charitable towards his relatives in times of need, in better times also lavish towards others. For the glory of God and the benefit of the church he bequeathed one hundred pounds to the School situated in Shadwell towards the catechesis of the boys in the Anglican church. Having done good to everyone, especially to the family of believers, he reaped reward in his own time, as someone who did not fail.

'Go, Reader, and do likewise.'

Nathaniel Resbury was born in 1643, the son of Richard Resbury, a non-conformist vicar. He received his training in Cambridge and Oxford before advancing to a number of clerical appointments, most notably rectorship of St Paul's, Shadwell (Middlesex) in 1689 and, as mentioned in the inscription, becoming chaplain in ordinary to King William and Queen Mary in 1691.

Described in the inscription as an orthodox, popular preacher as well as a prolific publisher of his writings, Resbury preached in London at Whitehall, St Paul's, and Charterhouse (see inscription 37), among other places.

Resbury's wife Mary, whom he had married in 1691, died only a short time before him. They had no children, allowing Resbury to bequeath significant sums of his estate in order to support charitable causes related to his lifelong beliefs and convictions. We can see these spelled out in the inscription, followed by the now-familiar exhortation of the reader to follow the deceased's example. (You can see similar examples in inscriptions 17 and 40.)

48. Commemorative Plaque for William Keate

This white monumental plaque, resembling a shield, is mounted on the south wall at the entrance of St Laurence's church and is currently not easily accessible due to the position of the modern gallery that houses the church office.

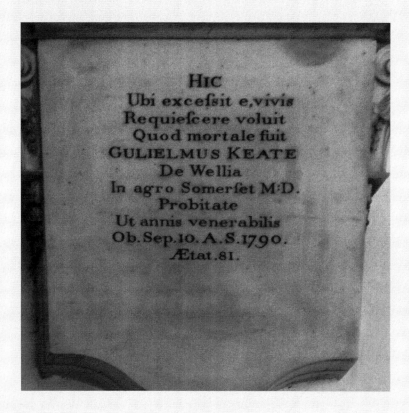

Hic
Ubi excessit e vivis
Requiescere voluit
Quod mortale fuit
Gulielmus Keate
De Wellia
In Agro Somerset M(edicinae) D(octor)
Probitate
Ut annis venerabilis.
Ob(iit) Sep. 10 A(nno) S(ancto) 1790
Aetat(is) 81.

'Here, after he departed from the living, wanted William Keate of Wells in the county of Somerset, MD, to rest what was mortal, venerable in probity and age. He died on the 10th of September, 1790, aged 81.'

William Keate has been described as the founder of the Wells branch of the Keate family – a family that included, among other notable people, John Keate, headmaster of Eton and Canon of Westminster.

William Keate was three times mayor of Wells, and is recorded as an apothecary there. He retired to Reading after the death of his wife in 1781.

Official records mention one William Keate involved in an undue election and return to Wells in 1766, where he is listed as 'Senior Master of said city', who 'was not the proper Returning Officer at said Election.'

If this is indeed the same William Keate that is mentioned in the inscription, his self-professed *probitas venerabilis*, his 'venerable probity', should perhaps be queried!

Reading's Fading Memory

Anamnesis and Amnesia – Recalling and Forgetting

Several inscriptions included in this book are now in a deplorable state of preservation. Particularly obvious cases are the two gravestones of Reading dignitaries in St Laurence's churchyard (43 and 44). They are but one manifestation, however, of the shameful state of some of Reading's historic monuments.

The epigraphic record of a place, the monuments and landmarks with their inscriptions, not only preserve collective memory – they constitute it. The gradual disappearance or removal of an important part of the public record reflects a community's readiness or inclination to forget and to suppress their historical roots. In that regard, Reading's history is crumbling away, and sometime soon many memorial sites and places of collective remembrance will have reached a stage that is beyond repair.

While the pitiful state of preservation and the damage to some of Reading's inscriptions are regrettable, in the grander scheme of things, these are by no means the worst things that can happen to monuments. All the inscriptions in this book, in one way or another, were at the heart of a little story, an episode in history, that gave a glimpse into the diverse, rich heritage of Reading. But what if the monuments, with their texts, are not preserved or recorded in any way? The answer is simple: what could not be preserved, and what has not been recorded, has been consigned to collective forgetting – collective memory's evil twin.

Lost Memory, Lost Identity?

Forgetting tends to be a gradual process; details are no longer remembered, biased interpretations turn into commonly accepted views, cause and effect get blurred, context that was too obvious be recorded at the time suddenly is no longer understood.

In the case of Reading's inscriptions – Latin or not – the process of an ever more disintegrating memory, alongside a loss of collective identity, can be traced in some detail.

The following four inscriptions have one thing in common. Their current fate is unknown – they may or may not still exist. They are reported in old (otherwise reasonably reliable, if sometimes somewhat inaccurate) histories of Reading and its monuments. Yet they are either no longer in the places where they originally belonged, leaving no information on their current position, or are, in fact, gone for good.

49. Gone Forever ... Or Not?

The sixteenth-century funerary inscription of one Thomas Justice was located 'On a plate fixed in a grave-stone lying near the south entrance into the chancel' of St Laurence's church. The inscription reads:

En Thomas Justice, quodam qui rexerat istud
Templum, sub gelido conditur hoc tumulo.
Dum vixit, Christi cultor fuit optimus ille,
Sacri mysterii verus amator erat.
Cujus nunc animo concedas, Christe, redemptor,
Molliter in gremio posse latere tuo.
Hic die Januarii 12, A(nn)o 1535
diem clausit extremam.

'Behold Thomas Justice, who once was in charge of this church, is buried underneath this chilly tomb. While alive, he was the best worshipper of Christ, a true lover of the Holy Mystery. Allow his soul now, Christ, Redeemer, to be able to hide comfortably in your bosom. He concluded his final day on January 12th, 1535.'

It is unclear whether or not this monument and inscription for Thomas Justice, once vicar of St Laurence's, still exists. Many other metal plates have been removed from monuments in this church, and it is entirely possible that this one was among them. The fact that this inscription is still reported in the early nineteenth century gives some hope. The space 'near the south entrance into the chancel', however, is now covered with new flooring, making it impossible to verify the continued existence of this rare example of an early sixteenth-century Latin inscription from Reading.

What is even more of a loss is that the first six lines of this inscription constitute a poem in elegiac distichs – an important addition to the number of late medieval and early modern Latin poems recorded on monuments in St Laurence's church (see inscriptions 36 and 38, above).

50. Gone, Found, Gone Again ... Or Not?

The idea of funerary monuments being re-used for profane purposes may seem rather shocking – something permanent like death seems to deserve eternal respect, at least to a Western European mind. The truth, however, could not be further from that. Metal plaques have a material value, and have consistently been 'recycled' with little or no respect for the dead. One such story has already been captured with the metal plaque that contains texts 37 and 38. The same is true for gravestones, which make excellent building material, not least due to their often sizeable dimensions and plain, rectangular shapes.

A particularly interesting example is the funerary inscription of one Charles More, 'on a black marble gravestone on the north side of the altar' of St Laurence's church. The stone was decorated with the arms ('a chevron between three heathcocks') and the crest ('a blackamoor's head') of the deceased. The inscription has been reported in old sources as follows:

M(emoriae) S(acrum).
Carolus Morus
publicus auctoritate regia notarius
supremae curiae admiralitatis Angliae
pro-registrarius, honestissimus
vir charitate insignis, et amico fidus
sub hoc marmore, spe resurgendi
sepultus jacet.
Vitam hanc caducam, secundo die mensis
Octobris, anno salutis restauratae 1673
pro beatiori in coelis mutavit.

'Sacred to the Memory. Charles More, Notary Public, by royal authority, Deputy Registrar of the High Court of the Admiralty of England, a most respected man of outstanding charity and faithful to a friend, lies buried under this stone, in the hope of resurrection. He exchanged this feeble life, on the second day of October in the year 1673 of our redemption, for a more blessed one in Heaven.'

The whereabouts of this inscription is now unknown, and has been unknown for a long time. At one point, however, it did resurface, in a most unlikely place – Southcote Manor (see inscription 27). During the demolition of this structure, originally a medieval fortified manor house, workmen unearthed the inscription as part of the building material. The same text was reported, except that the year of Morus' death has been read as 1675.

51. An Ever-Changing Urban Space: the Blagrave Church Walk

Reading's landscape is ever-changing – old buildings disappear, new buildings surface – and anyone who has not been to Reading for a decade is likely to find parts of the town that they will not recognise. All too often this is at the expense of historic buildings, but that situation is not a new one.

In the late 1860s, for example, a structure once described as 'a handsome portico called the church-walk' by Charles Coates in his *The History and Antiquities of Reading* (1802), was pulled down, much to the annoyance of many locals at the time. This structure, built in 1620 and funded from the estate of John Blagrave (see inscription 27), was an arcade attached to the south side of St Laurence's church, six arches long and open to Market Place. At some stage, it contained the Borough's stock and ducking stool, and there are surviving ancient drawings of St Laurence's that give an impression of this addition to the church building. The following inscription is reported on the outside of Blagrave's piazza:

Johannes Blagravius,
generosus, mathesiosque
encomiis celeberrimus,
libras C ad ambulacrum
hoc extruendum dedit, quod
opus major burgensesque (piae
beneficii hujus inter caetera
memoriae ergo) perficiendum
curarunt,
Febr(uarii) 1, 1619.
Reparatum & adornatum
Anno 1680.

'John Blagrave, generous and most celebrated in the praises of Science, gave one hundred pounds towards the construction of this walkway – a work that the Mayor and the Burgesses (in pious memory of this benefaction as well as others) saw through to completion: February 1st, 1619. Repaired and adorned, AD 1680.'

The Latin of the inscription is somewhat challenging, and it may have been misread: the word *mathesiosque*, 'of Science', is particularly curious, and other sources report it slightly differently, e.g. as *matheseos*. As the inscription has long since disappeared, together with the portico and any living memory of it, it is impossible to verify what it actually said.

52. Commemorating a Reading-born Classical Scholar and Typesetter

Finally, the following inscription is reported as once having been placed on a family tomb 'in the churchyard of St Mary, Reading'.

M(emoriae) S(acrum)
Parentum, fratrumque duorum,
quorum senior fuit
Guilielmus Baker,
Vir, litterarum studiis adeo eruditus,
Graecarum praecipue Latinarumque,
ut arti, quam sedulus excoluit
Londini,
(Ubi, in templo Dionysio dicato,
Ossa ejus sepulta sunt,)
Typographicae ornamento;
ac familiaribus,
ob benevolentiam animi,
Morum comitatem, et modestiam,
Deliciis et desiderio fuerit.
Omentum ejus auctum usque ad duodecim pondo
et ultra,
Literatos, auxilio eruditionis eximiae;
Sororemque, et fratres, et patrem senem,
Dulcibus illius alloquiis;
Ipsumque, mortem oculo immoto intuentem,
Vita privavit,
Die Septembris 29, 1785,
Aet(atis) 44.
E filiis, Johannes
hoc marmor
p(onendum) c(uravit).

'Sacred to the memory of the parents and two brothers, of whom William Baker was the elder, a man, erudite in the study of literature – Greek and Latin in particular – to the same extent that he was the pride of the art of typography, which he strenuously exercised in London (where in the Church of Dionysius his remains are buried); also he meant delight and desire to those close to him, due to the benevolence of his spirit, the pleasantness of his character, and his modesty. His omentum [or: bowels?] grew up to the weight of twelve pounds and more. He deprived the learned of the support of his outstanding education; his sister and his brothers, and his old father, of the sweet conversations with him; himself, facing death with a steady eye, of his life: on September 29th, 1785, aged 44. Of his sons, John had this stone produced.'

St Mary's churchyard nowadays bears little resemblance to its original design. Originally it extended further north. It was closed and partly ploughed under in the mid-eighteenth century, as a result of the increasing health hazard the many burials in above-ground vaults posed to the town.

The desperate situation of this churchyard was one of the factors that contributed to the creation of what is now known as Reading Old Cemetery, at Cemetery Junction.

Many tombs and headstones in St Mary's churchyard are in a state of serious disrepair, and many inscriptions are damaged and worn beyond recognition. There is now no trace of the inscription for William Baker or the family monument, and there is no record of what has happened to it.

In a town with a university that – quite rightly – takes pride in its Department of Classics, which has an illustrious history of more than one hundred years, as well as a world-leading Department of Typography and Graphic Communication, it seems particularly unfortunate that the memory of an intellectual ancestor, who combined both trades, should have disappeared.

Some Final Words

These four, now lost, inscriptions represent what was once a much richer tradition of Latin writing, documenting Reading's long, impressive, and varied history. These texts, in conjunction with all the others assembled in this little collection, are testament to just how much detailed historical knowledge and awareness of Reading's pedigree we risk losing, unless proper documentation and conservation takes place.

The fate of the lost inscriptions is a cry for a society that embraces and preserves the memory of those who once helped to build and shape it, and without whom – for better or worse – Reading would have been a very different place. The writing, quite literally, is on the wall! This, of course, does not only apply to the Latin inscriptions, but to all of Reading's crumbling, ill-preserved public monuments.

Finally, virtually all the inscriptions presented here are in the town centre or nearby. Yet many a Latin text can be found slightly further afield, in the churches of West Reading, and in the surrounding villages and towns of Berkshire and Oxfordshire. We need not be limited by the outline of the town of Reading; these inscriptions could, and should, be seen in a wider context. This wider context, too, invites contemplation and study – for personal gain as well as a deeper appreciation of local history, combined with a glimpse of the concerns of local people, from a variety of backgrounds, over the centuries.

Two Rivers Press has been publishing in and about Reading
since 1994. Founded by the artist Peter Hay (1951–2003), the press
continues to delight readers, local and further afield, with its varied list
of individually designed, thought-provoking books.